D1642606

WOODWORK

JOHN BOWLER

MINI · WORKBOOK · SERIES

MURDOCH
B O O K S

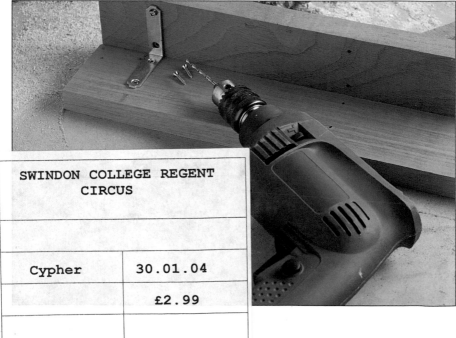

CONTENTS

A tenon saw (top) and an electric drill (bottom)

Setting up your workshop

A functional workshop is one that suits your needs, with sufficient work space, storage, electric power, light and ventilation. You will need room to move around your project, and remember you have to get it out of the door when it is completed.

LIGHTING

The work area must be well lit as poor lighting can lead to poor work. Fluorescent lights are best because they give a wide spread and provide a brighter output than conventional light bulbs, but always have at least one conventional (tungsten) lamp if you are working with moving machinery. Place lights so they are either directly over the workbench or to one side. Never place lighting so it shines in your face or behind you, as this will cast shadows on your work.

VENTILATION

Adhesives and paints can give off fumes, so plan the position of doors and windows to maximise cross-flow ventilation. This helps to disperse fumes (and dust), and it also helps adhesives and paints to dry. When you are working with timber, the air should be dry to prevent the timber warping or swelling.

ELECTRIC POWER

Ensure you have enough electric sockets, that they are conveniently placed around the work area and are protected by a residual current device (RCD) for safety. Any electrical installation work and wiring should be done by a qualified electrician.

WORKBENCH

Whilst an old table may be strong enough for small projects, you will need a strong bench for most woodworking. The bench should be about 85 cm (33½ in) high, with the legs braced to prevent spreading. The top should be of thick timber able to withstand blows, especially near the front edge. A thinner timber can be used at the back or middle to form a well where tools can be safely placed.

A portable folding workbench may be an option if space is a problem. It can be folded away when not needed and carried to the work site. The top is split in two halves which can be moved in and out to operate as a vice and can hold tapering workpieces.

Accessories for the workbench include adjustable bench stops for planing against, bench hooks to aid with cross cutting, a tool well, a drawer for storing tools or hardware and a woodworking vice. This differs from an engineering vice as it holds the workpiece alongside the bench, not above it, and has timber jaws to protect the workpiece surface. A low saw horse is also useful.

Keep a fire extinguisher and first-aid kit at hand for emergencies. Remember, good housekeeping plays an important role in safety.

STORAGE

Correct storage and care of tools will keep them in good condition. Tool racks or 'shadow' boards will protect them and help you keep track of them. Many tools come in a storage box when purchased. Even if it is cardboard, it will serve well for some time. If tools are not going to be used for a while, put them away, especially at the end of the day. A light coating of oil will prevent rust.

Keep hardware in its packaging until required—it is designed to protect the fittings and keep the parts together. Keep screws and nails in a box, clearly labelled.

BASIC TOOL KIT

There is an enormous range of tools available but you can build up your kit gradually, purchasing tools as the need arises. For best results, always buy recognised brands. A few basic tools are all you need to get started:

- claw hammer (570 g/20 oz)
- smoothing plane (No. 4)
- marking gauge
- combination square
- steel tape (3 m/10 ft)
- three bevelled-edge firmer chisels (10, 18, 25 mm)
- panel saw
- tenon saw
- nail punch
- set of twist drills
- set of screwdrivers (slotted, Pozidriv, Phillips)
- oilstone
- sanding block
- variable-speed electric drill
- jigsaw

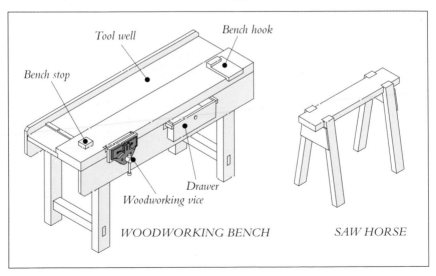

Bench hook

Tool well

Bench stop

Woodworking vice

Drawer

WOODWORKING BENCH

SAW HORSE

Chisels

A woodworker's chisel is a hand-guided cutting tool used to shape timber by paring away waste. It is also used to finish joints and to make recesses to receive hardware. Chisels are manufactured from fine-grained tempered steel and are bevelled on one end to produce a cutting edge. They range from 3–50 mm (⅛–2 in).

FIRMER CHISEL

This is a strong chisel used for general work and to remove large amounts of material. The blade is comparatively short and thick and may be square or bevel-edged. A firmer chisel can be driven by hand or hit with a mallet. The bevelled-edge firmer chisel is the more useful as it can be used for 'undercutting'—for example, on dovetail joints.

USING A FIRMER CHISEL

When chiselling, always keep the job secure in a vice or cramps, and never have your hands or any part of your body in front of the cutting edge. Ensure the chisel is always kept sharp (see the box on page 22 for the correct way to sharpen it).

1 To cut a recess with a firmer chisel, first make saw cuts, put the job in a vice, hold the handle in one hand and strike it with a mallet, removing the bulk of the waste.

2 Turn the job round and repeat from the other side, gradually levelling the housing. Turn the chisel over (bevel up) and hold it between thumb and fingers to guide the cut. Pare away the waste and smooth the bottom by moving the chisel from side to side in a slicing action.

PARING CHISEL

This chisel is used for light work, finishing off joints or anywhere where a fine degree of accuracy is required. The blade is long and thin

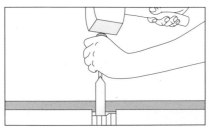

1 To remove the waste from a deep recess or housing, use a firmer chisel and strike it with a mallet.

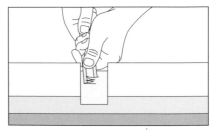

2 To level the bottom of the slot, hold the chisel in both hands and move it from side to side in a slicing motion.

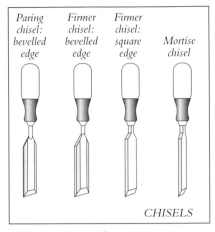

Paring chisel: bevelled edge | Firmer chisel: bevelled edge | Firmer chisel: square edge | Mortise chisel

CHISELS

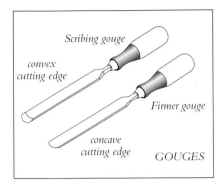

Scribing gouge
convex cutting edge
Firmer gouge
concave cutting edge

GOUGES

with the edges either square or, more commonly, bevelled. This chisel should only be driven by hand—one hand applying pressure to the handle while the other holds the blade and guides the cut.

MORTISE CHISEL

For extra-heavy work, this chisel is ideal. It has a square edge and a thicker blade than other firmer chisels and the blade tapers along its length. It is used for cutting mortises and levering out the waste. It may be driven by hand or struck by a mallet.

GOUGES

Gouges are similar to chisels, but have a curved cutting blade.

• Firmer gouges are ground on the convex (outside) face and used for detailed carving and hollowing out shapes and designs.

• Scribing or paring gouges are ground on the concave (inside) face and used for cutting around curved shapes such as mouldings.

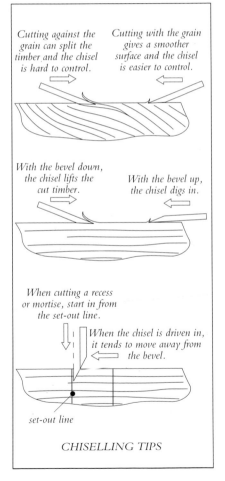

Cutting against the grain can split the timber and the chisel is hard to control.

Cutting with the grain gives a smoother surface and the chisel is easier to control.

With the bevel down, the chisel lifts the cut timber.

With the bevel up, the chisel digs in.

When cutting a recess or mortise, start in from the set-out line.

When the chisel is driven in, it tends to move away from the bevel.

set-out line

CHISELLING TIPS

Drilling tools

Most woodworkers use electric drills, but there are hand-operated types that may be used if electric power is not available. All drills are used in conjunction with interchangeable drill bits.

BRADAWL

A bradawl is used to make a hole to help start the thread of a screw. Place the flat edge across the grain in the desired position and force it into the timber with a back and forth twisting motion to cut the fibres.

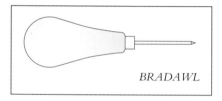

BRADAWL

HAND DRILL

The hand drill is used with twist bits up to 8 mm in diameter. It drills either timber or light metal (use a centre punch with metal). There is a larger hand drill called a breast drill.

To drill a hole, hold the top handle with one hand and apply pressure straight down. If you tilt the tool as you drill, the bit may break.

When drilling hardwood, the bit may clog up with shavings. To clear the hole and bit, move the drill in and out a few times.

HAND BRACE

This tool, with its larger cranking action, provides greater leverage for drilling through timber. It normally has a ratchet action, which allows you to drill in confined spaces as the brace can rotate in either direction by moving the collar on the crank which engages the ratchet wheel.

The chuck jaws are generally slotted to hold both parallel and tapered shank bits. When inserting a bit, turn the outer case of the chuck until the bit will fit between the jaws. Place the bit well down in the

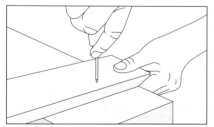

To use a bradawl, place the flat edge across the grain and force it into the timber with a twisting motion.

To use a hand drill, hold the handle with one hand and apply moderate pressure straight down.

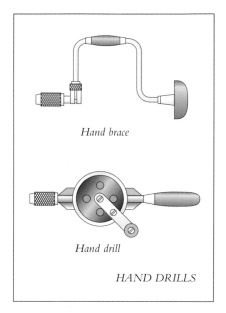

Hand brace

Hand drill

HAND DRILLS

centre of the chuck. Tighten it with the bit held central and firm.

To use the hand brace, centre the bit and apply pressure to the head of the brace. Rotate the crank clockwise. Check the bit is at 90 degrees to the surface. Drill the hole until the point of the bit just comes out the other side. Continue rotating the crank in the same direction without any pressure and pull back.

This will remove the waste from the hole. Now turn the workpiece round and drill in the same way from the other side, using the small hole made by the pointed centre as the guide. This will avoid any breaking out of the timber on the far side.

DRILLING AT AN ANGLE

To help maintain the correct angle and ensure the bit starts in the right place, cramp a guide block (made from a piece of timber with the correct hole in position) to the work. A depth stop may also be used to ensure the hole is the correct depth.

MAINTENANCE

Keep drill mechanisms free from grit and dust. Dust in the gears or bearings will make them stiff to operate. A little lubricant may be needed.

DRILL BITS

• Wood-cutting (Auger) bits are used mostly in the brace. They are used for boring deep holes with and across the grain. The sharp point of the bit has a screw thread that guides it and helps pull it through the workpiece.

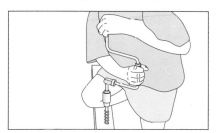

To use a hand brace with a bit, apply pressure to the head of the brace and rotate the crank clockwise.

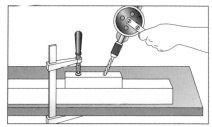

To drill a hole at an angle, use a guide block drilled at the correct angle. Cramp it to your workpiece.

Auger bits can have a straight-shank, or one with a single or double twist ('Jennings pattern'), and are fitted with side cutters (spurs) which cut the fibres off around the outside edge of the hole and provide a clean finish, especially important in cabinet work and when drilling softwoods. A twisted shank carries the waste timber out of the hole.

Flat augers without spurs are often referred to as speed or spade bits. They are used for fast cutting and leave a rough-edged hole. They must be used in an electric drill.

• Expansion bits are used in a brace for cutting large or odd-sized holes. They have the same cutting action as augers, but can be adjusted to bore

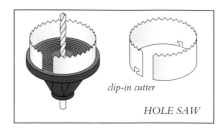

clip-in cutter

HOLE SAW

any size hole from 12–75 mm (1½–3 in). Large holes can also be made with a cylinder-shaped cutter called a hole saw, which is fitted to an electric drill and has a guiding twist drill bit.

• Twist drill bits are mainly used for metal, but they also work well in timber. They can be fitted to hand drills or electric drills. The straight shank must be held firmly in the chuck or it may slip and break.

• Countersink bits are used to recess the head of a screw into timber. There are two main types. The rose bit is used in hardwood and the snail bit in softwood. These bits are used by hand or in a brace. Special bits can also be used in electric drills for metal and timber. Only light pressure is normally required to countersink the hole.

• Dowelling bits come in the three main dowel sizes (6, 8 and 10 mm) and have a centre point and two 'spurs' to ensure a clean hole and to prevent them wandering off centre.

• A combination bit drills a pilot hole, screw clearance hole and countersink in one process. Some are restricted in depth but others are adjustable. A separate bit is required for each size (gauge) of screw.

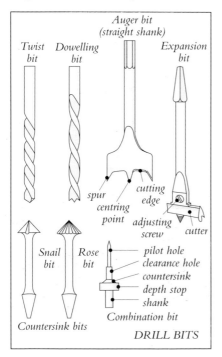

DRILL BITS

Files and rasps

Files are used to shape and finish timber as well as other materials such as metal and plastics. They come in a wide range of types.

TYPES

Files and rasps come in a variety of different shapes, of which the flat, round and half-round are the most useful for woodworking.

The teeth can be single or double cut. Single-cut files have teeth in one direction only; double-cut ones have two rows of teeth crossing. Woodworking files have coarser teeth than those used for filing metal.

Rasps have even coarser teeth and are used predominantly for rough cutting or shaping of timber.

A Surform file, available in a range of shapes, has a detachable serrated and perforated blade (fine-cut or standard) and is a very quick way of removing material.

USING A FILE OR RASP

1 To cross-file wood or metal, keep the file flat on the surface. Applying

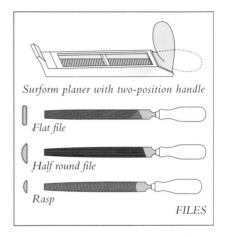

Surform planer with two-position handle

Flat file

Half round file

Rasp

FILES

slight downwards pressure, push the file forward with slow even strokes the full length of the workpiece. Do not apply pressure on the return as this will result in excessive tooth wear.

2 To draw-file, hold the file at 90 degrees to the surface and move the file back and forth along the surface. This produces a smoother finish.

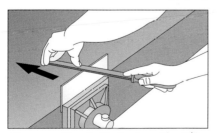

To cross-file, hold the handle of the file in one hand and steady it near the tip of the blade with the other.

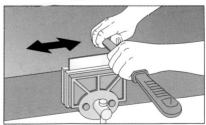

To draw-file, stand at the end of the job. Holding the file at 90 degrees, move it back and forth.

Gauges

The marking gauge is used to mark lines parallel to an edge or face into the surface of timber. Use it only where the timber is to be cut, never on a finished surface.

MARKING GAUGE

The marking gauge has two main parts—the stem, which has a steel pin or spur near one end, and the stock, which slides along the stem and is secured with a thumb screw.

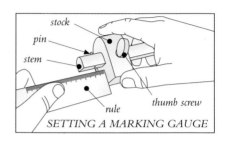
SETTING A MARKING GAUGE

To set a marking gauge, loosen the screw a little, slide the stock along the stem the required distance from the pin and partly tighten. The distance is best measured with a rule. The setting can be adjusted by tapping either end of the stem on the bench. Tighten the thumb screw and recheck the measurement.

Hold the gauge firmly, with the stem resting on the surface of the timber and the stock against the edge. Rotate it towards you until the pin touches the timber. Press lightly on the gauge and slowly push it forward so the pin marks the surface.

MORTISE GAUGE

The mortise gauge is similar to a marking gauge but has two pins for marking mortises and tenons.

PENCIL GAUGE

A line can be drawn parallel to an edge using a pencil gauge, which does not score the surface. Either run one of the fingers of the hand in which the pencil is held along the edge of the timber, thus maintaining the distance required, or use a pencil and rule or combination square.

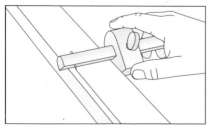
To mark a line parallel to an edge, hold the gauge firmly and push it forward so the pin marks the surface.

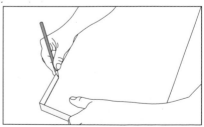
To draw a parallel line using a pencil, run one of the fingers of your hand along the edge of the timber.

Hammers, punches and nails

Two hammers form an essential part of any woodworker's tool kit: the claw hammer and cross-pein hammer. Both are used to drive in nails.

HAMMERS

The size of a hammer is determined by its head weight. The hardened face is slightly convex (rounded) so it is easier to strike a nail and prevent the hammer marking the work badly.

• Claw hammers have claws at the back of the head. They can be pushed firmly under the head of bent or unwanted nails to lever them out. The most useful size for woodworking is 450–570 g (16–20 oz). Claw hammers can have timber (normally hickory) handles or steel or glassfibre handles covered with a rubber grip.

• The Warrington or cross-pein hammer is used for light joinery work, to start small nails or panel pins. It is useful for nailing into corners. A smaller type (also known as a pin hammer) is used for panel pins plus small brads and tacks. These hammers range in size from 100–400 g (3.5–14 oz).

MALLETS

The wooden mallet is used to drive chisels and to assemble joinery work where a tool or the hammer would damage the surface of the workpiece.

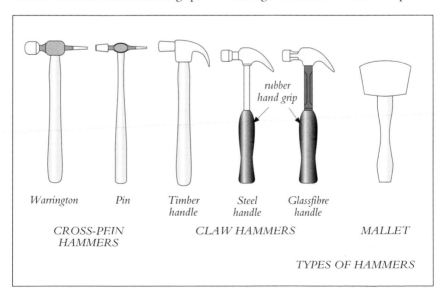

Warrington   Pin   Timber handle   Steel handle   Glassfibre handle

rubber hand grip

CROSS-PEIN HAMMERS   CLAW HAMMERS   MALLET

TYPES OF HAMMERS

A rubber-head mallet may be used to knock joinery together but not for striking chisels or other tools. Take care using these mallets as they may bounce back and cause injury.

USING A HAMMER

1 Keeping a straight wrist, hold the hammer near the end of the handle. With your other hand, hold the nail steady and rest the head of the hammer squarely on the nail head. The handle should be horizontal when the nail is vertical.

2 Tap the nail lightly to get proper aim and to start the point of the nail. Using wrist, elbow and shoulder action, continue to hit the nail squarely on the head. Sharp, glancing blows may bend the nail. Moderate force will drive the average nail into most timber with three to four blows. Use a nail punch to drive the nail home if required.

Never use the side of the hammer for striking nails. Keep the face of the hammer clean and bright so the head will not slip off the nail and damage the workpiece or your fingers.

PURCHASING A HAMMER

Choose a hammer to suit most of the jobs you do. It should not be so heavy that you need muscles of steel to use it, or so light that you have to hit nails too often to drive them in.

On a claw hammer, look for claws that have a sharp vee for a tight fit around the nail. Ensure the head is firmly attached to the handle. Check the balance. If the hammer feels comfortable and you can swing it easily, it is probably right for you. If in doubt, be guided by your retailer.

NAIL PUNCHES

A nail punch is a tapered, hardened piece of steel used to drive the nail below the surface of the timber.

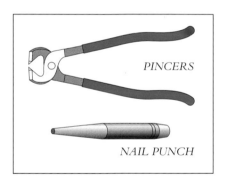

PINCERS

NAIL PUNCH

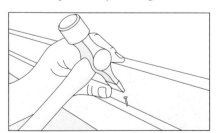

The flattened tip of a cross-pein hammer makes it useful when nailing into a corner or other tight place.

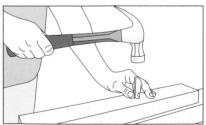

To start a nail, tap it lightly with the hammer while holding the nail steady with your other hand.

When new, the tip is concave (cupped) to fit the nail head and prevent it sliding off. There are different tip sizes for different nails.

To use the punch, first hammer the nail to within 2-3 mm (⅛ in) of the surface. Grip the punch firmly with thumb and forefinger. Rest the tip on the nail with the index finger pressing against the side of the punch ensuring the punch is directly in line with the axis of the nail. Use the hammer to strike the head of the punch to drive the nail 2–3 mm (⅛ in) below the surface.

EXTRACTING NAILS

The position and size of the nail will determine the extraction process. Long nails may be pulled from the work with a wrecking bar (also known as a crowbar or case opener).

When using a claw hammer, ensure the claws are pushed firmly under the head of the nail. Pull the handle until it is nearly vertical. Unnecessary force may break the handle. To increase the leverage and relieve the strain, place a piece of timber under the head and continue.

This will also prevent damage to the surface of the workpiece.

Pincers may be used to draw out small nails. Place the jaws around the head of the nail and lever it out. A piece of timber will increase leverage and prevent bruising the workpiece.

NAILS

Nailing is the quickest and most economical method of fastening timber together. Today, most nails are made from wire, usually mild steel, although other metals are used for specific situations (for example, copper nails for boat building). Most nails are left plain, but they may be hot dip galvanised, or nickel-, zinc- or cadmium-plated for use in areas of high moisture. Galvanised nails are for exterior use.

Nails come in a wide variety of head shapes for particular purposes (see Table on page 16). Some heads (for example, on lost-head wire nails and panel pins) are designed to be driven flush with or below the surface. Other types of nail include staples, escutcheon pins, cut brads and corrugated fasteners.

Once started, drive the nail in with sharp blows, using wrist, elbow and shoulder action.

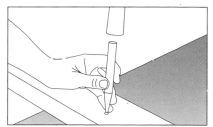

Use a nail punch to drive the head of the nail below the surface. Steady the punch on the head with one finger.

NAILS	
HEAD TYPE	PURPOSE
Flat head (round wire nail)	For joining thin materials to timber and softwood frames. The width of the head gives greater holding power. 25–150 mm (1–6 in) long.
Lost head (normal or oval)	For general purpose use in construction or cabinet making. Same sizes as flat head.
Cut clasp nail	Used in rough carpentry for joining timber together and also for joining timber to masonry. Because of its shape, it rarely splits wood; a similar nail is used for holding down floorboards. 32-100 mm (1½–4 in) long.
Ring shank nail	A round wire nail with raised ridges in rings along its length. Used specifically for fixing man-made boards where the rings help pull the boards together and prevent the nail being pulled out. 20–100 mm (¾–4 in).
Panel pin	Small, slender nails with a conical-shaped head for finer work. They leave a very small hole when punched. 10–50 mm (⅜–2 in) long. A thinner variety called a veneer pin is also available.

The point of a nail is pyramid shaped to force the fibres apart.

The thickness or wire gauge of a nail is normally stated in millimetres. The shank may be square or round. For greater holding in softwood, end grain or chipboard, use an annular, helical or twisted shank.

When ordering nails, state the length and gauge in millimetres, head type, material the nail is made from and the quantity in grams or kilograms. A typical nail order would be 2 kg of 100 mm mild steel flat-head wire nails.

The length of a nail is important to gain the maximum hold in the timber. When nailing across the fibres, the nail should be 2–2½ times the thickness of the timber and when

Use the claws on the hammer to extract a nail, placing scrap timber under the head to increase leverage.

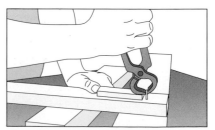

A nail can also be extracted using pincers, but again use scrap timber for leverage and surface protection.

nailing into end grain it should be 2½–3 times the thickness.

NAILING METHODS

Face nailing and skew nailing are the two most common methods of nailing timber together.

FACE NAILING

Face nailing means nailing through the face of the timber. Do not nail too close to the edge or use nails that are too thick as this may split the timber and reduce holding power. Nails rely on friction for their holding power—the greater the friction, the greater the hold.

For greater strength, you can 'dovetail' the nails. Drive the nails in at an angle towards the centre of the timber, staggering them to minimise the risk of the timber splitting.

When nailing close to an edge or end, use a thinner size of nail. To reduce splitting near an end, turn the nail upside down, place it in the correct position and give it a tap. This will flatten the point of the nail and form a 'cup' to receive the nail head in the surface of the workpiece.

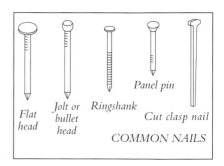

Flat head   Jolt or bullet head   Ringshank   Panel pin   Cut clasp nail

COMMON NAILS

Turn the nail over and drive it in the normal way around. In timbers such as hardwood it is a good idea to drill a pilot hole first. To create it, drill a hole slightly smaller than the nail through the face of the top piece and just into the top of the bottom piece. Then hammer in the nail.

SKEW NAILING

Skew nailing is used when you need to nail through the edge of a timber, where otherwise you would need a very long nail. Drive the nail in through the side of the timber at an angle of about 45 degrees. Stagger the nails and drive them in from both sides of the timber. This method of nailing is used extensively in construction work.

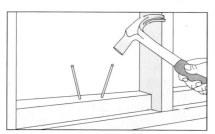

Dovetail nail by driving the nails in at an angle towards the centre of the timber and staggering them.

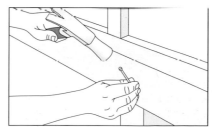

To skew nail, drive the nail in through the side of the timber at an angle of about 45 degrees.

Spirit levels

The traditional spirit level is used to check whether a surface is horizontal or plumb (vertical). The body of older levels is made from timber, but newer ones are aluminium or plastic.

PARTS OF A LEVEL

The body of the spirit level has a central vial used to check that surfaces are horizontal. The vial is a glass or plastic tube filled with fluid and a vapour (or air) bubble. Two graduation lines on the vial are spaced to suit the length of the bubble. When the spirit level is correctly set, the bubble rests exactly between these lines.

USING THE LEVEL

The surface to be levelled should be flat so the spirit level will not rock. Place the spirit level in the centre and adjust one end of the workpiece so that the bubble is between the lines. The bubble rises to the high end.

When you think the surface is level, turn the spirit level around end to end and place it back in the same position. Check the bubble again. If the spirit level is accurate, the reading will be the same. If not, the tool itself may require adjusting.

For levelling over larger areas, place a straight-edge (for example, a piece of timber with both edges perfectly straight and parallel) along the workpiece. Use the spirit level in the centre of the straight edge. Over considerable distances, a more accurate method is the water level. This is a clear plastic tube filled with water and is often used for levelling around corners.

CHECKING VERTICALS

To test work for plumb, the spirit level has vials at the ends. Place the spirit level in the centre of the workpiece and check the bubble as before.

Another method for testing for vertical is with the plumb bob. A plumb bob is a shaped metal weight attached to a string. When it is suspended from the top, the weight holds the string vertical.

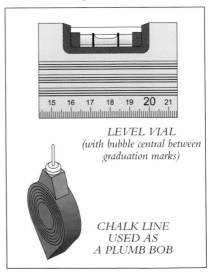

LEVEL VIAL
(with bubble central between graduation marks)

CHALK LINE USED AS A PLUMB BOB

Planes

The plane is used to produce a smooth surface on timber before it is sanded. Depending on the type of plane used, the finished surface may be flat, curved or moulded. Most planes are similar in use although they may differ in appearance.

TYPES OF PLANE

The main types of plane with adjustable cutters are the smoothing plane (the most common), the try plane (the longest) and the block plane (the smallest). Others have specialised uses. Each has a sole (base), a handle and a cutter (plane iron).

• Smoothing planes are widely used in woodworking for final finishing. A typical size is around 25 cm (10 in) long and 50 mm (2 in) wide. The blade does not extend the whole width of the sole (making rebate and shoulder cutting impossible). Jack planes are similar, but have longer soles, giving greater accuracy on longer workpieces. If sharpened correctly, a smoothing or jack plane will produce a flat, even surface ready for final sanding.

• Try planes are ideal for large surfaces. They are used for planing the edge off long boards to be joined or for large surfaces such as table tops which must be perfectly flat.

• Block planes used with one hand and the cutter set at a lower angle are very handy for small, fiddly jobs and for trimming end grain.

• Rebate planes are used to produce or clean up rebates. The cutter comes right to the edge of the sole and there are two cutter positions.

• Hand routers (router planes) are used for cutting or cleaning up the bottom of grooves, recesses and housings.

• Spokeshaves may have either a flat or round face and are used to smooth concave or convex shapes.

• Shoulder planes are used for cleaning up the shoulders of large joints and for cutting rebates (the cutter comes right to the edge).

• Plough planes are for cutting grooves and rebates whilst being guided by fences and depth stops. Combination planes (for mouldings) are similar.

USING A PLANE

1 To plane the surface of timber, secure the timber on the bench. For wide timber, use a bench stop or a block that is slightly thinner than your job, nailed to the bench. For narrower timber, use a vice. Set the plane to take off a fine shaving and place it flat on the surface with the cutter off the end of the timber.

2 Press down on the front of the plane and push forward slowly, taking a fine shaving from the end of the timber. As the plane passes over

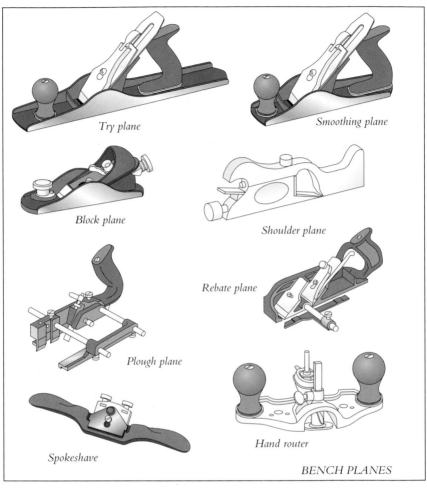

Try plane

Smoothing plane

Block plane

Shoulder plane

Rebate plane

Plough plane

Spokeshave

Hand router

BENCH PLANES

To start planing, stand with your weight on your back leg and exert pressure on the knob of the plane.

Push the plane forward, transferring pressure to the back of the plane and your weight to your front leg.

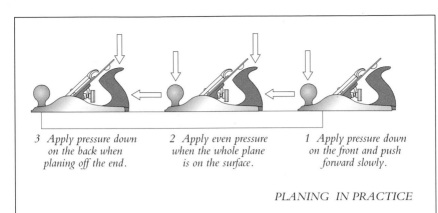

3 Apply pressure down
on the back when
planing off the end.

2 Apply even pressure
when the whole plane
is on the surface.

1 Apply pressure down
on the front and push
forward slowly.

PLANING IN PRACTICE

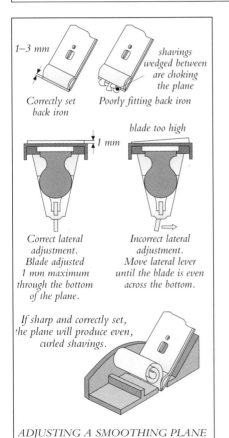

1–3 mm

Correctly set
back iron

shavings
wedged between
are choking
the plane

Poorly fitting back iron

blade too high

1 mm

Correct lateral
adjustment.
Blade adjusted
1 mm maximum
through the bottom
of the plane.

Incorrect lateral
adjustment.
Move lateral lever
until the blade is even
across the bottom.

*If sharp and correctly set,
the plane will produce even,
curled shavings.*

ADJUSTING A SMOOTHING PLANE

the timber, apply an even pressure to shave the entire length of the timber. When nearing the end, release the pressure on the front but maintain it on the back to plane the full length.

3 Place a straight edge across and along the timber to show up high spots. The edge of the plane may be used as a straight edge. Plane down the high spots, continually checking until a flat, even surface is obtained. Apply a face mark for identification.

4 To plane the edge requires more care. Keep the plane straight and square to the face. Sight along the edge of the timber and select the hollowed edge (it will straighten more easily than the rounded one). Use the longest plane possible. To guide the plane, place your thumb on top of the plane at the front with the tips of your fingers resting against the edge of the job. Plane the full length. Check from the face with a try square. Keep checking the edge.

5 To straighten end grain, hold the plane as before with a finger at the front to guide the plane, and work in from both ends towards the centre. (Otherwise the grain will split when you are planing off the end.) The plane must be sharp and set to take off a fine shaving.

SHARPENING PLANES AND CHISELS

Cutters become worn and chipped and require grinding and honing to restore them to good condition. A plane blade needs to be ground at an angle of 20–25 degrees and honed a further 5 degrees. For chisel blades the grinding angle is 25–30 degrees with honing a further 5 degrees.

GRINDING

If using a bench grinder, set the adjustable rest to the required angle. Hold the cutter, with the bevelled edge down, between the index fingers and thumbs of both hands. Position the cutter on the rest and move it from side to side across the full width of the cutting edge. Do not grind too quickly or leave the cutter in one position too long as this will burn the metal. Cool the cutter frequently in water. Keep fingers well away from the grinding wheel and wear safety glasses at all times.

HONING

To obtain a fine cutting edge, hone the cutter on a sharpening stone (oil stone). They come in coarse, medium or fine grade, or a combination. Choose a stone that is coarse on one side and fine on the other. Slip stones, with a rounded edge for inside curves, are also available.

Sharpening stones need to be lubricated with oil during use to prevent them clogging. Use a light general-purpose oil but do not use linseed oil as it clogs the stone.

Apply sufficient oil to the side of the stone you are using so it remains wet. Place the ground edge flat on the stone. Raise it slightly (about 5 degrees) and, applying an even pressure, move the cutter back and forth along the stone, ensuring the edge stays flat. Using a honing guide, fitted with rollers, allows you to set the angle exactly.

Lift the blade and check that a fine burr has appeared on the back edge: the blade is now sharp. This burr will need to be removed to produce a fine cutting edge. Lay the blade flat on the stone with the ground side up and move it backwards and forwards across the stone. The burr may also be removed by slicing the cutter through a piece of scrap timber although you will still need to rub the back of the blade on the stone.

Power tools

Power-driven tools make work easier for the woodworker as they will do the job in less than half the time of hand-operated tools. An increasing selection of battery-powered (cordless) tools, complete with a plug-in charger, are available, and can be safely used away from a source of electricity.

SAFETY

Portable power tools are dangerous. Use them with extreme care. Read the instruction manual supplied with the tool and follow these safety guidelines whenever you use them:

• Always follow the manufacturer's handbook regarding safety and correct operation.
• Never use faulty tools.
• Never use tools with faulty or frayed leads.
• Never lift tools by the lead or disconnect by pulling the lead.
• Keep leads away from cutters.
• Keep cutters sharp.
• Disconnect the power supply before adjusting the tool.
• Allow tools to reach full speed before working with them (apart from 'soft-start' electric drills).
• Never use tools in wet conditions.
• Avoid dropping tools.
• Never use tools for any purpose for which they were not designed.
• Wear appropriate safety clothing and equipment.

ELECTRIC DRILL

The most used power tool in the workshop is the electric drill. All drills are much the same, regardless of size and make. They have a motor, trigger switch and a chuck to hold the bit. Jaws within the chuck hold the drill bit in place and prevent it slipping when locked. Normally, the jaws are locked with the aid of a chuck key, turned clockwise to lock and anti-clockwise to unlock but 'keyless' chucks which you tighten by hand are becoming more common.

Most drills have a pistol-style hand grip with a trigger switch that can be locked on. Some are supplied with a second adjustable front handle, usually fitted with a depth stop.

The body houses the motor and at the front is the gearbox, which regulates the speed and functions such as hammer action.

BUYING A DRILL

When buying a drill, choose one that suits your needs. Cordless drills are handy but not as powerful as mains electric drills. A drill will be more useful if it has more than one speed—low speed for metal or masonry and a higher speed for timber. Variable speed control lets you select the speed for any job,

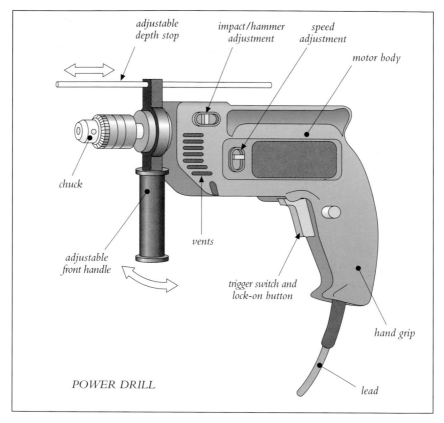

adjustable depth stop

impact/hammer adjustment

speed adjustment

motor body

chuck

adjustable front handle

vents

trigger switch and lock-on button

hand grip

POWER DRILL

lead

especially when using screwdriver bits. Some also have torque control, so there is more or less twisting force on the screw head.

The chuck size refers to the size of drill bit shank that will fit in the drill. Generally, the more powerful the drill, the bigger the chuck (a 500 watt motor could have a 10 mm chuck, a 700 watt motor a 13 mm chuck). Either of these would suit the average woodworker.

Impact drills or hammer drills are best for masonry. Unlike normal rotary drills, where the bit remains locked in the chuck and rotates, the bit in these drills vibrates in and out while rotating. The effectiveness of this action relies on the force you apply to the drill. This action may be disengaged to drill normally.

Some drills, especially battery-powered drills, have a reverse rotation for removing screws. Drills can be fitted with disc sanders or grinding wheels as accessories.

A vertical drill stand allows an electric drill to be held so that it drills holes straight and to a required depth. A lever moves the drill.

POWER DRILL HINTS

• Using a centre punch to create a starting point will prevent twist drill bits wandering.

• Keeping the drill running until it is removed from the hole will help clean out any waste. Move the drill back and forth while drilling masonry or hardwood to help clear the hole and drill bit.

• When drilling ceramic tiles, place masking tape over the area to be drilled to prevent the drill wandering. Never use the impact or hammer action on tiles or they will crack.

OPERATING THE DRILL

Select the appropriate bit for the job (see Drill bits on pages 9–10). Never use auger bits with a lead screw as they will jam and/or overload the motor. Instead, select spade bits that can be used on high speed. Always use tungsten carbide bits for masonry. They are made to withstand the pressure required.

When placing a drill bit in the chuck, ensure it is in the centre and turn the chuck key (or the chuck) until the jaws have tightened on the drill shank. Remove the chuck key.

Select the correct speed for the bit and job. Smaller bits require a higher speed than a bigger bit. The harder the material, the slower the speed.

When drilling holes over 8 mm in diameter, use a drill with a front handle for greater control and to help prevent injury should the bit jam.

Remember to secure your work in a vice or clamp and maintain a firm grip while you are drilling. Keep the drill at the required angle. Changing the angle while drilling may break the bit or make an irregular hole.

If drilling all the way through a piece of timber, clamp a block of scrap timber to the back of the job. This will help prevent the back splitting when the drill breaks through the other side.

CIRCULAR SAW

Circular saws are used to make straight cuts through timber, metal or masonry. They come in a range of sizes from 150–250 mm (6–10 in) the diameter of the blade governs the depth of the cut of the saw.

When purchasing a circular saw, think about the type of material you are likely to be cutting and select a saw that is able to cut through the material in one operation.

Saws generally come supplied with a combination blade for ripping or cross-cutting, although special ripping or cross-cutting blades are available. A blade with tungsten carbide tips will provide a cleaner cut and last much longer.

The saw is fixed to a base plate which can be raised or lowered to change the depth of cut. It is held by a locking lever or nut. The base plate may also be tilted up to 45 degrees to the side for angle (bevel) cutting. On top of the base plate is a fixed guard that covers the saw blade; beneath is

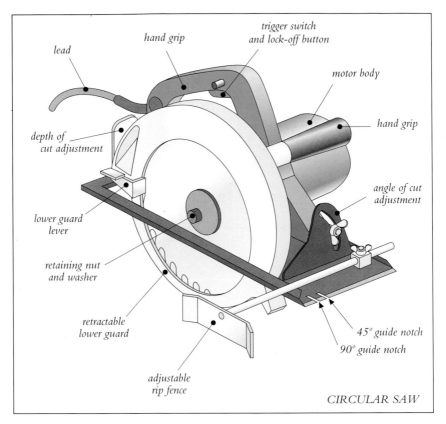

lead

hand grip

trigger switch
and lock-off button

motor body

hand grip

depth of
cut adjustment

angle of cut
adjustment

lower guard
lever

retaining nut
and washer

retractable
lower guard

adjustable
rip fence

45° guide notch

90° guide notch

CIRCULAR SAW

a retracting guard that must operate freely at all times as the saw moves through the work.

PREPARING TO CUT

Measure and mark the cutting line on your job. Fit the appropriate blade for the material you will be cutting. Set the depth to 5 mm more than the thickness of the material. For cross cutting, position the job on saw horses or other stable support with the waste side on your right, overhanging one end. This allows the weight of the saw to rest on the

material. The job must be held firm and this can be achieved by any of the following three methods:

• Hold the saw in your right hand

When cross cutting with a circular saw, use your knee to hold the work. Line up the notch with the line.

and place your left knee on the job.
• Clamp the material to saw horses.
• Nail blocks of timber to the saw horses on either side of the job to make a channel for it to sit in.

If the job is small, nailing it down while cutting will probably provide the greatest stability and safety.

For ripping timber, use the last two methods only—the timber will normally be too long and narrow for the first method.

When using your saw:
• Never wear loose clothing that may get caught in the saw.
• Remove all nails, bolts and grit from second-hand timber.
• Ensure the guard works properly.
• Never use a saw on which the blade has been damaged.
• Use the right sharp blade for the job.

CUTTING PROCEDURE
Stand slightly to the left of the job to avoid kick back. Secure the work (see above). If ripping material, use the rip fence supplied or clamp a straight edge to the job to guide the saw. Place the saw base plate flat on the surface of the material and line up

the notch at the front of the plate with the cutting line so the blade doesn't touch the material. The lock-off button has to be depressed before you can operate the main trigger switch.

Start the saw and allow it to gain maximum speed before steadily pushing it forward along the cutting line. Keep the base plate flat on the job until you have completed the cut and the waste has dropped. Turn the saw off and allow it to stop rotating. Check that the bottom guard has returned before placing the saw on the ground or bench.

CHANGING THE BLADE
Always unplug the saw before changing the blade. The saw blade is held in place by a retaining nut. To prevent the blade moving while you undo the nut, engage the locking device (if fitted) or place the saw on a piece of soft timber and push the blade into it until the teeth are embedded. Undo the retaining nut in the direction of the saw rotation and remove the old blade. Clean the washers and flanges and replace the blade in the reverse manner.

A circular saw is ideal for ripping timber. Here a rip fence is used to guide it.

To rip a board, clamp a straight edge to it and use that as a guide for the circular saw.

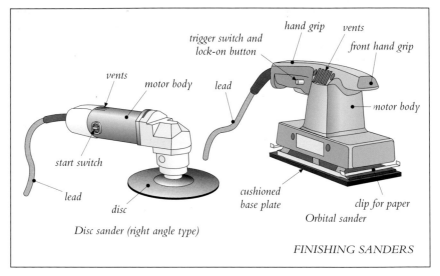

trigger switch and lock-on button

hand grip *vents*

front hand grip

vents *motor body* *lead*

motor body

start switch

lead

disc

cushioned base plate

clip for paper

Orbital sander

Disc sander (right angle type)

FINISHING SANDERS

MAINTAINING THE BLADE

Blades that are sharp are most efficient so keep them free of dust and timber resin. Sharpening blades, however, is probably best left to a professional, especially blades with tungsten carbide tips as they require special grinding. Talk to your local tool supplier to find a saw doctor.

SANDERS

Power sanders can be used to shape and remove timber, although to achieve a fine finish the work must be completed by hand sanding.

Disc and belt sanders remove large amounts of timber very quickly. With practice, you can use them to produce a large flat surface or curved work. A flexible disc attachment may be used with a power drill.

The most useful power sander is the finishing sander. The orbital or reciprocating action will produce a fine, flat surface that will need little hand finishing. It uses normal abrasive paper—either one half or one third of a full sheet.

The sanding paper is stretched across the base and held by spring-loaded clips. Take care when selecting the abrasive paper as coarse grades may damage the surface.

OPERATING THE SANDER

Start the sander before placing it on the job. This will prevent jumping

When using an orbital sander, use long, overlapping strokes forward and back, always along the grain.

which could damage the surface. Some sanders have a lock-on button so you do not have to hold the trigger on manually while you work. Hold the sander with both hands, one on the trigger handle and the other on the front handle. Place the sander flat on the surface and, with light pressure, guide it slowly backwards and forwards over the work. Too much pressure will wear out the abrasive paper. Keep the sander moving evenly. Do not sand too much in one place as this may create a depression.

Clean the sander regularly with a soft paint brush to remove dust.

JIGSAWS

Jigsaws are used to cut curves or to make a cut-out from the edge of a workpiece. By changing the blade, it is possible to cut a wide variety of materials. Jigsaws come in many designs, some with dual or variable speed. The smaller, light-duty saws are used for thin material such as plywood. Heavy-duty types can cut most material, from thin board or metal to thicker timber. Most jigsaws have an adjustable base plate for bevel cutting and come supplied with a ripping fence. The blade of a jigsaw moves up and down, with the cutting taking place on the upstroke (so any chipping occurs on the top surface); a pendulum-action jigsaw moves the blade away from the cut on the downstroke, giving faster cutting, less blade wear and an even better finish on the lower surface.

OPERATING THE JIGSAW

Secure the work as vibration is a problem, especially on thin sheet material. Select the appropriate blade and fit it. Blades are relatively

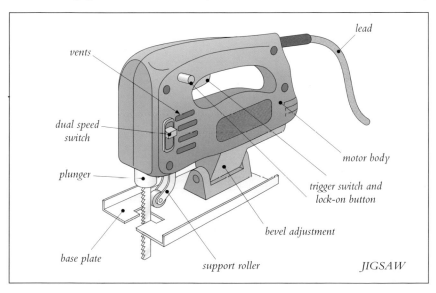

lead

vents

dual speed switch

plunger

base plate

support roller

motor body

trigger switch and lock-on button

bevel adjustment

JIGSAW

inexpensive to replace, so throw out blunt blades. If you have a dual-speed model, select the appropriate speed.

Mark the cutting line and place the base plate on the surface in line with it. With the blade just off the material, start the saw. With the motor at the correct speed, slowly push the saw with a firm forward motion. Never force the blade as it may wander or break. Keep a moderate downward pressure on the saw to stop it lifting from the surface.

On internal work, such as cutting a circular hole, draw the shape on the surface. Make a starting point by drilling a hole the size of the blade on the waste side of the line. Insert the blade in the hole and work towards the cutting line, gently turning the saw to follow the shape. A circle cutting guide may be purchased for your jigsaw.

On soft timber or thin material such as plasterboard, you can cut a hole without drilling a starter hole by plunge cutting. Rest the saw on the front of the base plate and tilt it forward until the blade clears the material. Turn the motor on and

gradually lower the saw into the material, maintaining firm pressure. Complete the cut in the normal way.

ROUTERS

The portable electric router can be used for cutting grooves, rebates and recesses or for shaping the edge of timber, using guides and fences.

There are more than 200 types of cutters, from straight to elaborate; some have ball bearing guides, some don't. These are mainly for cutting along the edge and require a guide to run the router against. A guide fence or wheel can be attached to the base plate of any router. Without a guide, the rotation of the cutter and the timber grain makes it hard to control the router. Cutters are high speed steel or tungsten carbide tipped.

OPERATING THE ROUTER

Fit the appropriate cutter and fix any fences or guides to the router or work. Start the motor and allow it to gain full speed—be careful as the power of the motor may twist it out of your hands. Rest the base plate on the workpiece. To obtain a clean cut,

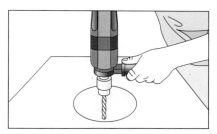

To start a hole for a jigsaw, use a power drill with twist bit to drill a hole on the waste side of the line.

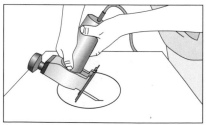

On thin material the cut can be started by plunging the jigsaw blade into the material at an angle.

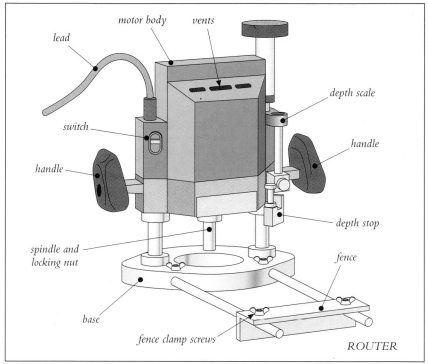

lead

motor body

vents

depth scale

switch

handle

handle

spindle and
locking nut

depth stop

fence

base

fence clamp screws

ROUTER

the router should run at high speed. If it is too slow it may create friction and burn the material. Hold on to the router firmly with both hands. Move it into the timber to make the cut, working from left to right so the cutting edge is fed straight into the timber. Keep it firmly pressed against the guide or fence to eliminate any chatter. Do not try to cut the whole depth in one go; do it in stages.

When routing all sides of a piece of timber, rout the end grain first to prevent splitting.

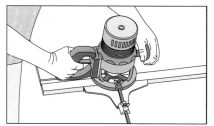

The easiest way to cut a groove is to use a router. Here a fence is attached to keep it going straight.

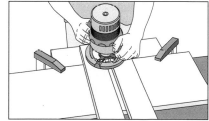

A groove can also be cut using a router and a jig. The gap in the jig is the width the groove will be.

Sanding blocks and paper

Sanding blocks and abrasive-coated paper (commonly called sandpaper) are used to produce a fine, smooth finish on timber.

SANDING BLOCKS

Sanding blocks are small pieces of cork or other soft material around which a piece of abrasive paper is wrapped. Using one not only saves your hands, it helps maintain an even pressure on the sanding paper and avoids rounding the edges of your workpiece.

When you are ready to sand, wrap a piece of abrasive paper the same width as the block around it and place the block on the surface of the timber at 90 degrees to the direction of the grain. With an even pressure, move the block back and forth.

Hold the sanding block at 90 degrees to the grain or a splinter may be caught between the paper and the block. Circular or cross sanding scratches the workpiece.

To clean up timber that has a moulded shape, it may be necessary to use a block with a matching shape, otherwise the shape may be distorted when sanding by hand.

SANDING PAPER

The coat or grade of sanding paper comes in fine, medium or coarse and may have a numbered coding. The higher the number, the finer the abrasive, for example, 40–60 is coarse (for shaping timber), 80–120 medium, 150 and above fine (for giving a final finish). These coats are applied in different densities. On 'open coat' the abrasive is spaced further apart and so reduces clogging. 'Close coat' has abrasive closer together for a finer finish.

When sanding, start with a coarse grade and work through to a finer grade to produce the required finish. Fold or tear the sandpaper into a manageable size and replace it when it becomes worn or begins to tear.

If the paper clogs, it may be cleared by shaking or tapping the back to loosen the dust. For an even finer finish, raise the grain by wiping it over with a damp cloth. When it is dry, give a final sand with fine paper.

When sanding end grain, the fibres will sometimes lean in one direction (rub with your finger to determine the direction). Sand only in this direction, not back and forth.

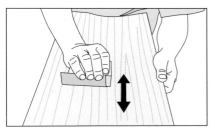

When sanding hold the block at 90 degrees to the grain and move it back and forth, applying even pressure.

Saws

A saw is used mainly for cutting solid timber or panel products, although there are other saws for different materials. There are traditional hand saws as well as power saws to suit different jobs.

PARTS OF A SAW

The traditional hand saw has a wood or plastic handle at one end of a thin, flexible tapering blade, varying from 550–700 mm long (22–30 in).

The teeth vary in size and shape according to the type of saw. The size is quoted as the number of teeth per 25 mm (or inch), so a 7-point saw has seven teeth per 25 mm. The fewer the teeth, the faster and rougher the cut. Each tooth has been bent out 'set' on alternate sides of the blade to provide a 'kerf', or clearance for the saw. 'Handpoint' saws have heat-treated teeth which last much longer, but cannot be resharpened.

HAND SAWS

• The rip saw is the largest handsaw used for cutting along the grain, a technique known as ripping. The teeth have 3 to 6 points and the blade is about 650 mm (26 in) long.

• The cross-cut saw is used for cutting across the grain. The teeth cut like a series of knife blades that sever the fibres. They range from 5–9 points and the blade is 600–650 mm (24–26 in) long.

• The panel saw is used for cutting panels, manufactured boards such as plywood and chipboard, and finer work. It has 9–11 points; the blade is about 550 mm (22 in) long.

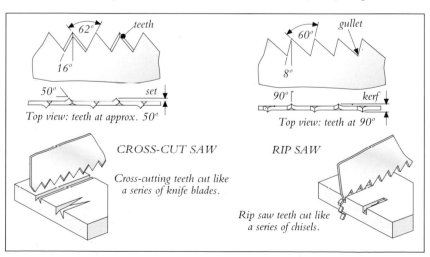

teeth

62°

16°

50°

set

Top view: teeth at approx. 50°

gullet

60°

8°

90°

kerf

Top view: teeth at 90°

CROSS-CUT SAW

Cross-cutting teeth cut like a series of knife blades.

RIP SAW

Rip saw teeth cut like a series of chisels.

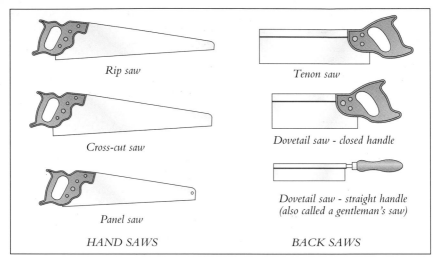

Rip saw

Tenon saw

Cross-cut saw

Dovetail saw - closed handle

Panel saw

*Dovetail saw - straight handle
(also called a gentleman's saw)*

HAND SAWS

BACK SAWS

BACK SAWS

These saws have a straight blade with a reinforced back of steel or brass over the top edge. This adds stiffness and weight to the saw. The teeth are cut and set as on a panel saw, only finer. These saws have between 10 and 14 points and cross-cut teeth.

• The tenon saw is the most common back saw and is widely used for cutting most types of joint. If it is the correct size, it can be used in the angled slots of a mitre box (see page 37) for cutting mitres or in the straight slot, to give a square cut.

• The dovetail saw is used for cutting with or across the grain on very fine joints or small beads. Smaller than a tenon saw, it has three handle types: closed, open or straight.

CURVE-CUTTING SAWS

• The coping saw has a spring steel frame with two levers for altering the blade position, and a handle that turns to lock the blade in position. This saw is used for cutting intricate shapes, including inside and outside curves. Keep the adjusting levers parallel while maintaining the correct tension on the blade.

The blade should never be forced as it is easily broken (replacement blades are inexpensive). It is placed in the frame with the teeth towards the handle—the cutting action relies on pulling, not pushing as with other saws. Keep the blade square to the workpiece and do not cut too quickly.

When using a panel saw hold it at a low angle to reduce splitting and steady the work with your knee.

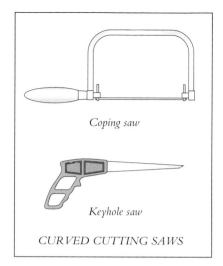

Coping saw

Keyhole saw

CURVED CUTTING SAWS

- The fret saw is similar, but has a large frame and the blade is generally not adjustable. The blade is thin enough that it can be turned in any direction without any adjustment.
- The keyhole or padsaw has a narrow, tapered blade designed to cut holes in a panel. When cutting internal curves, drill a hole through the work on the waste side of the line to get the saw started.
- Other saws used for curved work include bow saws for larger curves and, of course, powered jigsaws.

HOW TO USE A SAW

All timber, whether being ripped or cross-cut, must be held firm. This applies whether you are holding the work by hand, vice or cramp, and your job must be supported during the sawing process. Work only on a steady surface and avoid excessive vibration. Use saw horses to support longer pieces, with only as much timber overhanging as you need.

If the saw cuts badly or slowly, it is blunt. Never force the saw. Jamming a saw into timber will distort the blade and render it useless. Watch for nails or screws. The saw will cut them, but you will then have to resharpen the saw.

Most woodworking saws have one handle so one hand is left free to hold the work. To steady your work when cutting on a saw horse, rest a knee or foot on top of the timber. If cutting in a vice or using cramps, the job should be held as close as possible to where it will be cut to avoid the saw jumping, which makes cutting difficult and dangerous.

Hold the saw with your forefinger pointing towards the blade. This

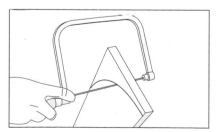

The coping saw with its fine blade is used for cutting curves. The work is held steady in a vice.

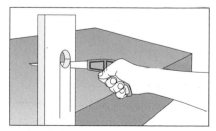

A keyhole saw is used for cutting inside work. Drill a hole on the waste side of the line to get it started.

gives better control. To start a cut, mark the cutting line with a pencil and place the saw on this line at a low angle while holding your other hand over the end of the timber next to the line. Rest your thumb against the blade to guide the saw.

Pull the saw backwards a little to make a slight cut, then push forward the same length. Repeat a few times, gradually increasing the length of stroke. Once the cut is 20–30 mm long, bring your hand back to steady the timber. Raise the angle of the saw to about 45 degrees for cross-cutting or 60 degrees for ripping.

Move into a comfortable position and use full, steady strokes with only light pressure. Let the saw do the work. Position your body so that the saw, forearm and shoulder are at 90 degrees to the work and you can see the line to be worked. If the cut runs out of square (under cut) your piece may end up the wrong size.

To prevent the saw binding when ripping timber, place a thin wedge in the cut to keep the kerf open. Do not twist off the waste with the saw blade or the underside may split off.

CROSS-CUTTING

When cross-cutting, support the weight of the offcut when you near the end of the cut. Lower the angle of the saw and cut steadily.

When cross-cutting a veneer surface board, lower the angle of the saw to minimise the amount of break out on the bottom of the board. To cross-cut small sections of timber mouldings and joints, hold the timber against a bench hook or in a mitre box and cut with a tenon saw.

When using a tenon or dovetail saw, keep your thumb against the blade and raise the handle so the saw cuts the far edge first. Draw the saw back to start the cut, gradually lowering it as it cuts.

To cut square, square a line around the timber and cut down about 3–4 mm on all sides. Then keep turning the timber, cutting a little deeper on each side in turn. The saw will follow the cuts already made. Alternatively, score a fine line around the timber with a sharp knife or chisel, then remove a small section of timber on the waste side to form a groove in which the saw can run.

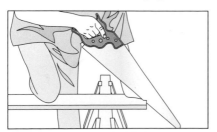

To start a rip cut, hold the saw at a low angle and pull it back. Use your knee to hold the work steady.

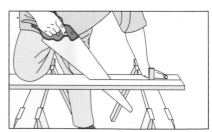

Raise the angle of the saw and use long, steady strokes. A thin wedge in the cut will stop the blade binding.

Timber mitre boxes are used to cross-cut timber at 45 and 90 degrees. They are used in the same way as a bench hook but you don't need to use your thumb to guide the cut as the box will do it. Adjustable metal mitre saws with their own blades, may be used to cross-cut timber at any required angle.

CURVE CUTTING

For curve cutting, place the timber vertically in the vice as low as possible. In some cases the timber can be held horizontally with cramps: even if it has to be moved during cutting the sawing will be easier. Start the saw cutting horizontally and follow your set-out lines. Keep the saw square to the face of the timber.

For internal cuts, drill a hole through the timber on the waste side of the line. Push the blade through and, if using a coping saw, replace it in the frame. You may have to turn the blade within the saw frame.

MAINTAINING SAWS

Generally, the only parts of the saw requiring maintenance are the handle

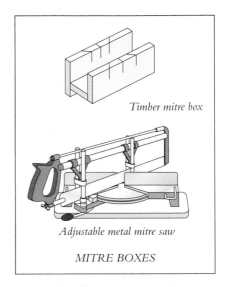

Timber mitre box

Adjustable metal mitre saw

MITRE BOXES

and teeth. After some use, the teeth will become blunt and need resharpening and/or setting. This should be done professionally: ask your local hardware store to recommend a saw 'doctor'.

When it is not in use, stand a saw on its handle leaning against the bench or saw horse. When you have finished using it, protect its teeth by placing a protective sleeve over them. A piece of plastic pipe with a split down one side is quite effective.

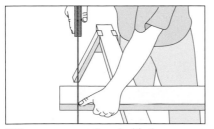

When cross-cutting hold the saw at 90 degrees to the surface and use your thumb to guide the blade at first.

When finishing a cross-cut lower the angle of the saw and support the end of the work with your other hand.

Scrapers

Woodworking or cabinet scrapers are flat pieces of tool steel with a cutting edge that will remove a very fine shaving when pushed over the surface of timber.

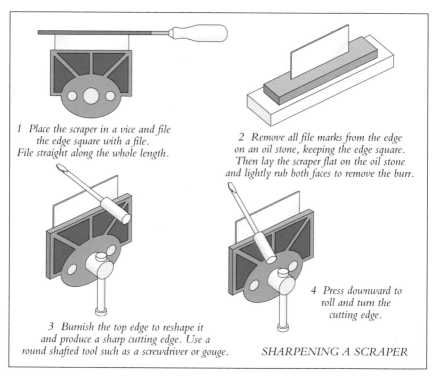

1 Place the scraper in a vice and file the edge square with a file. File straight along the whole length.

2 Remove all file marks from the edge on an oil stone, keeping the edge square. Then lay the scraper flat on the oil stone and lightly rub both faces to remove the burr.

3 Burnish the top edge to reshape it and produce a sharp cutting edge. Use a round shafted tool such as a screwdriver or gouge.

4 Press downward to roll and turn the cutting edge.

SHARPENING A SCRAPER

CABINET SCRAPERS

Hold a cabinet scraper with both hands. Place fingers over the face and press the thumbs firmly into the back of the scraper, flexing it slightly.

To use the scraper, place the edge on the surface of the timber at a low angle. Firmly pushing it forward, remove a shaving. Adjust the angle of the movement as necessary.

Hold a cabinet scraper with both hands, press your thumbs against the back of it and push it away from you.

Screwdrivers and screws

There are different types and sizes of screwdrivers and each one will only do a small number of specific jobs successfully. Using the wrong screwdriver may result in damage to the job, the tool and the operator.

TYPES OF SCREWDRIVER

Screwdrivers may be hand operated or power driven. Hand-operated ones have a timber or plastic handle, a steel shaft and a blade or tip at the end. A power screwdriver or drill has a screwdriver bit inserted into it.

To cover household tasks, you will need five or six screwdrivers of varying size, blade and tip types. They should include the three basic types of tip:
• slotted, with a flat blade for standard headed screws;

• Phillips, with a cross-shaped tip for screws with recessed heads (mainly found on machine screws and self-tapping screws);
• Pozidriv, similar to Phillips but much more common on wood screws, ground at a different angle to allow greater force to be applied to screws without damaging the head.

Phillips screwdrivers may be used on Pozidriv-head screws, but take care not to damage the head as the recess in the head and tip do not match exactly. Never use Pozidriv screwdrivers in Phillips-head screws as they will damage the head or tip.

Screwdrivers may be purchased individually or in a kit. They are selected by the length of the shaft and size of the blade or tip. Slotted screwdrivers are measured by the width of the blade in millimetres. Phillips and Pozidriv screws are measured by the diameter of the shaft, which is quoted as a number from 1 to 3 (3 being the largest). The table on page 41 shows a basic kit.

A screwdriver blade or tip should fit the screw head exactly, reaching the bottom of the slot or recess. If it is too wide, it will damage the surrounding timber when driven in,

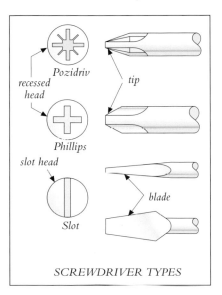

recessed head

Pozidriv

tip

Phillips

slot head

Slot

blade

SCREWDRIVER TYPES

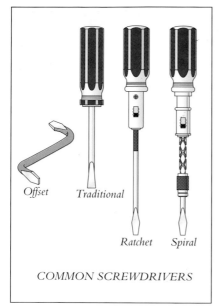

Offset   *Traditional*

Ratchet   *Spiral*

COMMON SCREWDRIVERS

and if too narrow, it may damage the slot or recess, making the screw difficult to drive.

Common screwdrivers are:
- traditional, with a wood or plastic handle;
- ratchet, which can be used without altering your grip;
- spiral, which turns the screw as the handle is pushed in a pump action;
- offset, which has a lever-type handle and is used in confined spaces.

Other specialised screwdrivers are available but they are not common.

USING A SCREWDRIVER

Using a screwdriver correctly needs practice. You may need two hands to get started: one on the handle and one steadying blade and screw. To avoid injury, never have any part of your body in front of the screwdriver.

Before inserting a screw, always make a pilot hole to guide it and relieve any friction. Failure to do this may result in damage to the screw and/or screwdriver.

When you have positioned the screw, place the screwdriver in the head in direct line with the screw, otherwise the blade may slip off. Apply an even, downward pressure while turning clockwise. Continue until the head is pulled up tight.

To loosen old screws clogged with paint or rust, first clean the heads to ensure the screwdriver will fit properly into the slot or recess. Place the screwdriver into the head and give it a light tap with a mallet to jar away any rust. This may have to be done several times while turning the screwdriver.

A range of screwdriver bits can be used in braces or variable-speed drills. Slotted bits are hard to control with either tool, so only use Phillips or Pozidriv bits.

MAINTAINING SCREWDRIVERS

Apart from a small amount of lubrication on ratchet types, there is

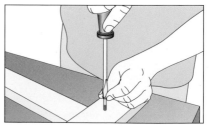

To insert a screw, hold the screwdriver in line with the screw and steady the head of the screw.

BASIC SCREWDRIVER KIT		
QTY	SIZE	LENGTH
1	4-6 mm slotted	150 mm
1	6-8 mm slotted	200 mm
1	8-10 mm slotted	250 mm
1	No. 1 Phillips	165 mm
1	No. 1 Pozidriv	165 mm
1	No. 2 Phillips	200 mm
1	No. 2 Pozidriv	200 mm

little maintenance required.

The blades on slotted screwdrivers should have cross-grinding marks for greater holding power. If they are burred or rounded, restore them with a file or grinder but ensure you shape both faces the same and that they are square so they fit the head of the screw correctly. Never overheat the blade as this will weaken the strength of the steel. These blades can be reshaped several times.

Phillips and Pozidriv tips require more care to restore as there are four sides to be shaped exactly the same. Hold the shaft in a vice and use a hand file. The angles on these tips will not withstand more than a few attempts at filing. You may find it better to replace the tool.

Screwdrivers are not levers or chisels and should never be hit with a hammer. Incorrect use can bend the shaft, damaging the blades or tips or cracking the handle. Shafts can be straightened but if you crack a handle you may find that it is cheaper and easier to replace the entire tool.

SCREWS

Screws give greater holding power than nails as the threaded shank cuts its way through the timber fibres. Screws are used to fix joints as well as to secure hardware and fitments. They are usually made from mild steel, brass or stainless steel and are available in a variety of finishes such as galvanised, bronze, nickel, cadmium and zinc plated. The heads may be slotted, recessed (Phillips or Pozidriv) or hexagon type.

When ordering screws, you will need to know the following:
• Purpose: the material you will be fixing to, such as wood or metal.
• Quantity: the number required. Screws are normally boxed in 100s or 200s, depending on size. Some suppliers sell smaller quantities in sealed plastic bags called 'blister packs' or on cardboard cards.
• Length: the amount the screw goes into the timber. Screws range from 6–150 mm ((¼–6 in).
• Gauge: the diameter of the shank given as a number. The higher the number the bigger the diameter. Screws range from 1 to 20.
• Type: head type as well as the type of drive. You may also need to state the thread required.
• Material: the metal the screw is made from plus any surface coating.

COMMON SCREW TYPES	PURPOSE
Countersunk head	Head finishes flush with or below the surface. For general timber work.
Round head	Head finishes above the surface. For thin sheet material and where head should be seen.
Raised head	Combination of countersunk and round head. For fixing hardware and where appearance is important. Can be used with cup washers for fixing thin sheets.
Long threaded	Countersunk embedding head; thread spaced apart for greater holding power. For chipboard.
Coach screws	Square or hexagonal head. For heavy work, such as fencing or pergolas.

The most common size for screws is from 12 mm (½ in) x No. 4 gauge to 100 mm (4 in) x No. 12 gauge.

An example of how to place an order for screws would be 100 only 50 mm x No. 8 gauge Pozidriv countersunk steel wood screws.

SELECTING SCREWS

You need to select a screw according to the type of material you will be joining. With softwoods you need to use a longer screw with a thicker gauge than you would need to get the same holding power with hardwoods. There is less holding power in end grain than cross grain so the screw will need to be longer.

Another consideration is the thickness of the two pieces of material being joined: you do not want the screw to come out the back of the workpiece. Whilst there is no hard-and-fast rule, the screw should be long enough to penetrate the bottom piece of timber by the thickness of the

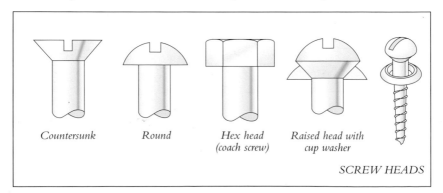

| Countersunk | Round | Hex head (coach screw) | Raised head with cup washer |

SCREW HEADS

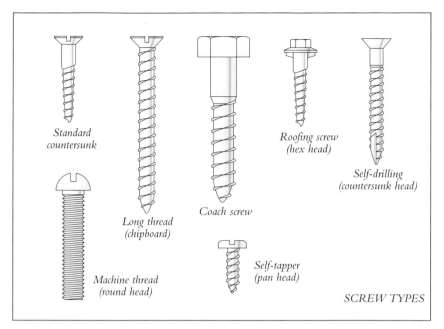

Standard countersunk

Long thread (chipboard)

Coach screw

Roofing screw (hex head)

Self-drilling (countersunk head)

Machine thread (round head)

Self-tapper (pan head)

SCREW TYPES

top piece, for example, to hold down a 25 mm piece of material, use at least a 50 mm screw.

BORING A HOLE

When you have selected your screw and a screwdriver that suits the size and type of screw, drill a clearance hole completely through the top piece of timber to match the diameter of the shank of the screw. On the bottom piece of timber, drill a smaller pilot hole at least half the depth of the clearance hole. This smaller hole gives the thread of the screw a firm bite.

If you are using a countersunk screw, the top of the hole will need to be countersunk to receive the screw head. Use a countersink bit attached to an electric drill or place

the bit in the clearance hole and turn it by hand. Twist it several times to create a recess for the head. Avoid countersinking too deep. Test the depth by inverting the screw and inserting the head into the countersunk hole.

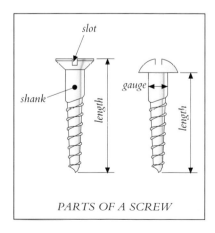

slot

shank

gauge

length

length

PARTS OF A SCREW

Squares

Components that are not square will not fit together neatly and the job will look rough. Always test them with a square.

TYPES OF SQUARE

• To use the traditional woodworking square (try square), hold the stock firmly against the workpiece with the blade over the face or edge to be tested. Sight between the blade and work. If the blade is not parallel to the surface, it is not square. Some try squares have a 45 degree angle on the stock near the blade for setting out and testing mitres. A square may be used to check internal and external corners.

• More versatile is the adjustable combination square. The blade length can be adjusted and secured in place by a locking nut. The stock may also be used to set mitres as it has a 45 degree shoulder at the top. The adjustable graduated blade may be used to test the depth of recesses or as a ruler. Most come with a levelling vial and a marking scriber. Many plastic-handled saws have the handle shaped so that it can be used (with the back of the saw) for marking out 45 and 90 degree angles.

• An adjustable sliding bevel may be used to set out or test a required bevel or slope on timber.

• For larger jobs, use the carpenter's (or roofing) square. It is made from a single flat piece of steel.

TESTING A SQUARE

For accurate work, a square should be 'square'. Be careful not to distort it and never use it as a hammer. To test the accuracy of your try square, make

> **HINT**
> Assuming the sides of a box or frame are parallel, you can test whether your job is square by measuring the diagonals. If they are the same, the job is square.

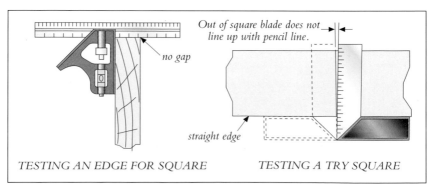

no gap

Out of square blade does not line up with pencil line.

straight edge

TESTING AN EDGE FOR SQUARE   *TESTING A TRY SQUARE*

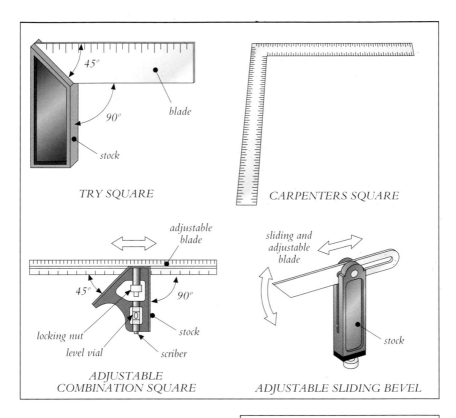

TRY SQUARE

CARPENTERS SQUARE

ADJUSTABLE
COMBINATION SQUARE

ADJUSTABLE SLIDING BEVEL

a line across the face of a straight piece of timber while holding the stock firmly against the edge. Turn the square over. If the blade lines up with this line, the try square is accurate.

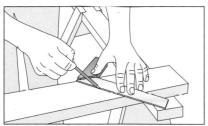

To mark a line at 45 degrees using a try or combination square, hold the stock against the edge of the timber.

OIL AND WAX

• A light smearing of oil can be used to protect tools from rust if stored for long periods.

• If a plane squeaks when in use, try a little beeswax or oil on the bottom. This may, however, be transferred to the work and it will need sanding before finishing.

• To reduce friction when using a saw, rub the side of the blade with light oil or candle wax.

• Wax or soap may be used on screws to reduce friction and make screwing them in easier.

Tapes and rules

Tapes and rules come in a wide range of shapes and sizes but only two are needed for most work: a folding rule and a steel tape.

TAPES

Steel measuring tapes have a flexible blade that is spring loaded to retract into the case. The case may also have a belt clip and a locking device to prevent the blade retracting. The sliding hook allows accurate internal and exernal measurement.

Tapes are usually marked in both millimetres and inches and range in length from 2–10 m (6–33 ft). Replacement blades and springs are available for good quality tapes.

By taking good care of your tape, you can lengthen its life:
• Keep it dry so the blade and spring do not rust.
• Never let the blade retract at speed as this may snap the hook rivets.
• Do not drop the tape as this may snap the spring, crack the casing or damage the hook.
• Do not bend the blade as this can split or break the spring steel.

MEASUREMENTS

In woodwork, measurements are taken in millimetres or metres, not centimetres. For example, a nail may be 75 mm, not 7.5 cm, and timber is purchased in 300 mm (or 0.3 m) increments, not 30 cm.

• Keep the spring lubricated with a light machine oil.

FOLDING RULES

Folding rules are made from boxwood or plastic with four sections hinged together with brass or stainless steel fittings. They are usually 1 m (39 in) long and graduated in millimetres and inches. Plastic rules are generally more durable.

Your rule will last longer if you don't whip it around or bend it excessively, as this places extra stress on the hinges. Always fold the leaves in the direction of the hinges.

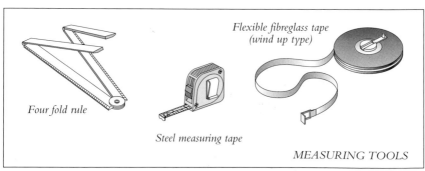

Four fold rule

Flexible fibreglass tape
(wind up type)

Steel measuring tape

MEASURING TOOLS

Timber

Timber is a renewable natural product that can be cut and moulded to virtually any shape or size.

SAWING METHODS

The two main methods used to convert a log into usable boards are plain sawing and quarter sawing. Plain (through) sawing is more common because it produces a large number of boards from a log, including a good number of wide ones. The boards have growth rings parallel to the face and the rings are prone to cupping or warping as each face shrinks at a different rate. These boards tend to cup away from the heart side.

Quarter sawing is less common as it produces fewer boards. These boards have growth rings at right angles to the face and are a higher quality with even shrinkage on each face. They are more expensive.

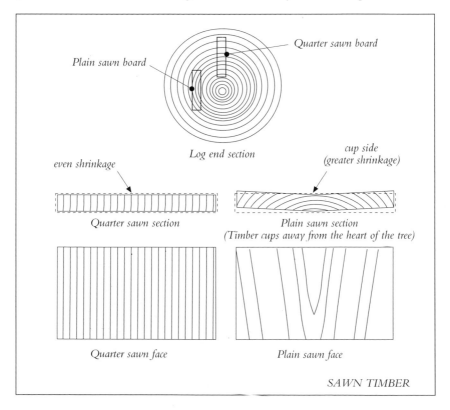

Plain sawn board

Quarter sawn board

Log end section

even shrinkage

cup side
(greater shrinkage)

Quarter sawn section

Plain sawn section
(Timber cups away from the heart of the tree)

Quarter sawn face

Plain sawn face

SAWN TIMBER

HARDWOOD OR SOFTWOOD

Timber is classified as hardwood or softwood according to its growth structure: it bears no relation to how hard the timber is. For example, balsa is classified as a hardwood but is very soft, whilst hard yew is a softwood. Hardwood trees have broad leaves, while softwood comes from cone-bearing trees such as pine and fir with needle-like leaves.

Hardwood is best suited to external work and construction as it withstands greater weathering than does softwood. Well-seasoned (dried) softwood is mainly used inside the home, but can be used outside if protected by paint, varnish or preservative stain. Both hardwood and softwood can be used for furniture if they are seasoned well.

Always wear a dust mask and goggles when using treated timber as the preservatives used can react with your skin or cause other illnesses. The offcuts of treated timber should never be burnt.

PURCHASING TIMBER

Timber can be purchased either sawn or planed. Sawn timber is rectangular or square and the surface will be rough: it is regarded as unfinished. Sawn timber is used for general building construction and is available preservative-treated for protection against rot and insect attack.

Timber used for most projects is planed timber. This means that it has already been machined once, but may need to be further smoothed by planing or sanding. Most planed timber is PAR (planed all round), though you may find some merchants supplying timber which has been planed on only two or three sides. Moulded timber has been machined to an specific profile.

The process of planing timber reduces the finished size of the actual timber. For example, a piece of sawn timber 100 mm square (its sawn size) will finish around 95 mm square when planed. You have to keep this in mind when planning your work.

Timber rarely comes supplied in the size required for a particular project. It may still need to be reduced further by cutting and/or planing. Your timber merchant may offer this service for an additional fee.

Timber is readily available in lengths ranging from 0.9–6 m in increments of 0.3 m. The thickness and width of timber range from 12.5–100 mm and 12.5–225 mm respectively. Although lengths, widths and thicknesses greater than these are available, they may have to be specially ordered and are expensive. If you need timber wider than 225 mm, you could use one of the man-made boards available (see Right) or join planks of timber edge to edge following the instructions on page 68. Alternatively, you may be able to buy laminated board (for example, Pineboard) where the supplier has already joined boards together like this. These are likely to give a better result than timber you try to join yourself.

SELECTING TIMBER

In theory, you should be able to select from a number of different timbers—for example, 'stress-graded' timber comes in different numbers according to its structural strength and there are different grades of timber according to its appearance, depending on the number of defects (see below) and how straight it is.

In practice, though, your choice will be limited to what your local timber supplier has available.

Apart from looking for defects, you will obviously want to think about the appearance of the timber—particularly if the surface is to be left unpainted. Look at how the grain runs (the straighter the better) and the number of 'knots' the timber has (these are the points where tree branches came off and can exude resin at a later date).

DEFECTS IN TIMBER

The grain in timber may be either wavy or ribbon, with knots and resin pockets. These may be regarded as defects or as features that can be worked and polished. Seasoning can also create defects in timber that will, in some situations, make working with it difficult (see diagram on page 50).

ORDERING TIMBER

When ordering timber, you need to provide the timber merchant with certain information if you are to get the timber you need. This consists of the following:
• the section width and thickness, for example, 100 x 50 mm
• the length, for example, 1.2 m
• the condition, for example, PAR
• the species, for example, pine
• the number of pieces

MAN-MADE BOARDS

Timber products such as chipboard hardboard and medium density fibreboard (MDF) were developed for reasons of economy. They are manufactured from forest thinning waste such as branches and sawdust, that would otherwise have been burnt and are either bonded together under pressure (hardboard and MDF) or held together with glue (chipboard). They are cheaper than solid timber and are available in large sheet sizes.

There is a variety of finishes available: plain synthetic or natural timber veneers, or plastic laminate and melamine. These products have no obvious grain, and most have an edge that can be machined to any shape although chipboard needs an edge finish such as veneer or edging strip.
• MDF is used in craft projects and for skirtings and architraves as it machines well and sands up to an excellent finish ready for painting. It does, however, contain chemicals that can cause skin problems for some people. Always work out of the sun, wear gloves and protect your eyes, nose and mouth from the dust.
• Take care when nailing or screwing near the edge of chipboard as it may split. Fixing into the edge of the board also creates a problem as the particles will pull out very easily.

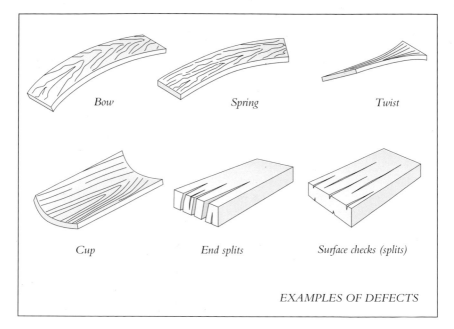

Bow

Spring

Twist

Cup

End splits

Surface checks (splits)

EXAMPLES OF DEFECTS

MDF and hardboard are less likely to be damaged in this way.

• Plywood consists of an odd number of veneers glued together, the number varying from three to thirteen. Alternate layers have the grain at 90 degrees, with top and bottom layers running in the same direction. Plywood is much stronger than chipboard, and nailing and screwing near or on the edge poses no problems. Cutters such as saws keep their edge longer with plywood than with MDF or chipboard.

• Blockboard consists of square long strips of wood, glued together side by side and sandwiched between two thin timber veneers. Usually the strips will be softwood, whilst the veneers will be hardwood (often birch). The result is stronger than natural wood (but not as strong as the same thickness of plywood) and large sheets are available.

FINISHING TIMBER

Any finish applied to timber is only as good as the preparation beneath. The timber must be seasoned or the paint or lacquer may peel, blister or crack. Any surface faults in the timber should be repaired before the finish is applied.

• Remove scratches with fine abrasive paper or use a scraper.

• Steam out bruises in bare timber by placing a damp cloth over the area and applying a domestic hot iron.

• Fill chips or cracks with slivers of matching timber glued down with PVA adhesive, or use a matching wood filler.

Timber joint construction

There are scores of joints that can be used to join timber. The skill is in fitting the pieces together precisely to form a joint that functions properly and is able to withstand the forces applied to it.

TYPES OF JOINT

There are three main categories of timber joint—box joints, framing joints and widening joints. Box joints are used for drawers and cupboard shelves, framing joints for windows and doors, and widening joints to join timbers for panels.

Many joints can be used for more than one purpose, for example, butt joints are used in all three categories.

PREPARATION OF TIMBER

Even planed timber may require some preparation.

• Cut the timber slightly over width and thickness to allow for planing. Do not cut the length yet.

• Choose the best side (face). Plane it the full length. Check it with a straight-edge. When it is straight, apply a face mark with a pencil.

• Plane the face edge. Check with a straight edge and square from the face side. Plane the cupped side to straighten it. Mark the face edge.

• Using a marking gauge, scribe a line for the thickness required all round. Plane to this line as necessary. Check with a straight-edge.

• Repeat on the side for the width.

Now set out for length and joints. Work from the face side and edge.

STEPS IN SETTING OUT TIMBER

Always take care when setting out the timber. Allow enough timber for waste from saw cuts, planing and joint construction. Work from the face side and edge marks. On frames and cupboards, keep these marks facing in for greater accuracy. To help sort out which piece goes with which, number them on the face side as you cut so side 1 goes with end 1.

If setting out identical parts, align them carefully and set out across all of them. This ensures the marks are identical on all. When setting out moulded or rebated sections ensure there is one left-hand and one right-hand section.

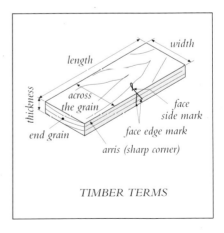

TIMBER TERMS

Butt joints

This is the simplest of all joints. It can be used in box, widening or framing construction.

CONSTRUCTION

Cut the ends of the two pieces square and place them together. Fix with screws or nails. Adhesive may be applied to the joint before fixing to increase its strength. Butt joints in framing may also be strengthened by fixing a nail plate or metal joint fastener over the outside, or a timber block may be fixed to the inside.

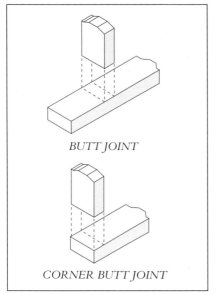

BUTT JOINT

CORNER BUTT JOINT

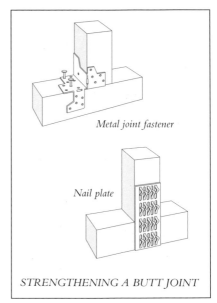

Metal joint fastener

Nail plate

STRENGTHENING A BUTT JOINT

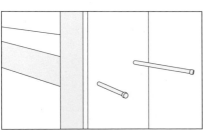

A butt joint can be fixed using dovetail nailing. Drive the nails in at an angle and stagger them.

Butt joints rely on fixings for strength.

Dowelled joints

Dowels may be used to add strength to a joint. They prevent the joint breaking sideways and rely on adhesive to hold it together. Dowel joints may be used in framing joints (furniture), box joints (cupboards) or widening joints (panels).

CONSTRUCTING A DOWEL JOINT

1 Accurately cut all components to size. Set out the position of the rail on the face side and edge of the stiles.

2 Mark the centre lines for the dowels at the ends of the rails. This must be at least half the thickness of the material in from each edge. For wide rails, more than two dowels may be required.

3 Lay the stiles and rail face side up on a flat surface, in their correct location. Using a try square, transfer the centre lines on to the stile. Number and mark each joint.

4 Square these marks across the face edge of the stiles and ends of the rails.

5 From the face side, gauge a line across the centre of the timber to cross the set-out lines. This represents the centre of the dowel holes.

6 Using a power drill or a hand drill with a special dowelling bit (6, 8 or 10 mm), drill the holes straight in all the pieces. Make sure the drill bit has a long centre point and clean cutting spurs. When drilling into cross grain the depth of the holes should be about two and a half times the diameter of the dowel and in end grain three times the diameter. Leave approximately 2 mm clearance at the bottom of each hole.

7 Lightly countersink the top of the dowel hole to remove any fibres. This also helps when inserting the

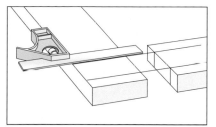

2 Mark the centre lines for the dowels on the end of the rail and use a square to transfer them to the stile.

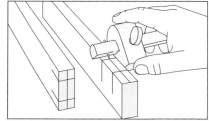

5 Gauge a line across the centre of the timber to cross the set-out lines and indicate the centres of the dowels.

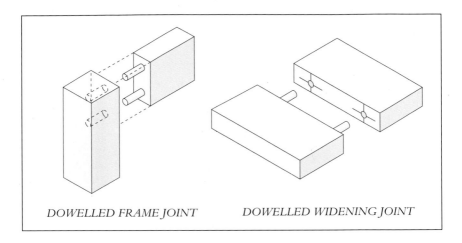

DOWELLED FRAME JOINT   *DOWELLED WIDENING JOINT*

dowel and provides an adhesive 'pocket' for greater strength.

DOWELS

Dowels should have grooves down the side to allow any extra adhesive to escape when the joint is assembled. If the dowels do not have a groove, plane one side flat to achieve the same result. The ends should be tapered (chamfered) to permit easier assembly and prevent the dowel tearing the inside of the hole. Again, if the dowels are not tapered, file or sand them to a tapered shape.

USING DOWEL CENTRES

Set out and drill the rails of the joint. Place dowel centres in the dowel holes. Line the rail up with the set-out lines on the stile and push together. The points on the centres will make small marks on the stile. Drill on these marks. An alternative way of locating the centres is to drill

holes in a guide block and clamp it in place as a guide when drilling.

USING A METAL DOWELLING JIG

A metal dowelling jig makes locating and drilling the dowel holes much simpler. In box joints, a dowelling jig can be used for the end grain but will not work on the face of the board.

1 Set out centre lines on the face of the material where the dowel holes are to be. Select the appropriate drill guide and place it in the jig.

2 Line up centring guide marks on the side of the jig and lock the sliding cradle in place.

3 Place the jig over the timber. Line up the centring vee with the centre lines of the dowel holes; tighten.

4 Fix the depth stop on the drill bit at the required length.

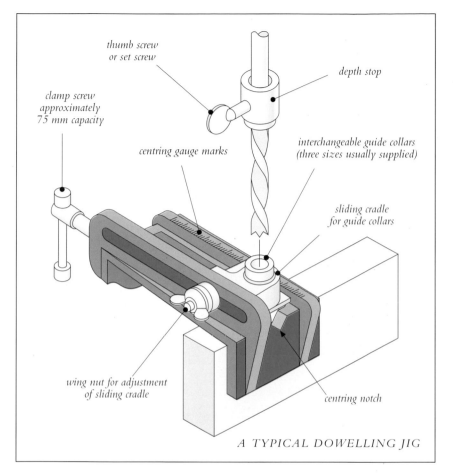

thumb screw
or set screw

depth stop

clamp screw
approximately
75 mm capacity

centring gauge marks

interchangeable guide collars
(three sizes usually supplied)

sliding cradle
for guide collars

wing nut for adjustment
of sliding cradle

centring notch

A TYPICAL DOWELLING JIG

WIDENING JOINT

To obtain a wider piece of timber, two pieces the same thickness may be joined edge-to-edge with dowels.

Hold the two pieces of timber face to face in a vice, with the ends carefully aligned. Square a line across the face edge to mark the centre line for each dowel. Gauge a line across each of the centre lines in the middle of each edge. Where these lines cross each other is the centre of the hole.

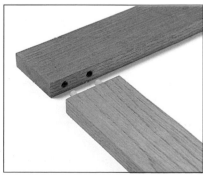

A dowelled joint is neat and strong.

Housing and rebate joints

A housing joint is used as a corner or intermediate joint where one board end meets the face of another. It is based on a butt joint with a shoulder to provide extra strength and is used in framing or box construction and for supporting shelves.

TYPES

The main types of housing joint are through housing and stopped housing joints (both of which are stronger than a butt joint), corner housing joints (used at a corner to form right angles) and stopped corner housing joints.

Corner rebate and stopped rebate joints are made in the same way but two-thirds of material is removed.

CONSTRUCTING A HOUSING OR REBATE JOINT

1 Set out the housing on the face of the material. The distance between the two lines is the thickness of the other piece. Square the lines across the face and down both edges.

2 Use a gauge to mark the depth of the housing between the lines on the edge. The depth is generally one-quarter to one-third the thickness of the material. Mark the waste.

3 Use G-cramps to hold the work down firmly. Saw the shoulders on the waste side of the line to the depth required. If it is a wide housing, make a few intermediate cuts inside the waste to help break the grain and make chiselling easier.

4 Chisel out the waste from both sides and check the bottom of the housing for flatness. A hand router may be used to level the bottom of the joint.

5 Test for fit. If the piece is too tight, it may need to be eased by planing or with a chisel. Check for square.

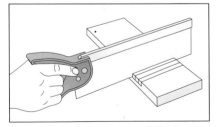

3 Cut on the waste side of the line to the depth line, making intermediate cuts in wider housings.

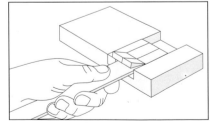

4 Use a chisel to remove the waste, working from both sides to ensure the bottom is level.

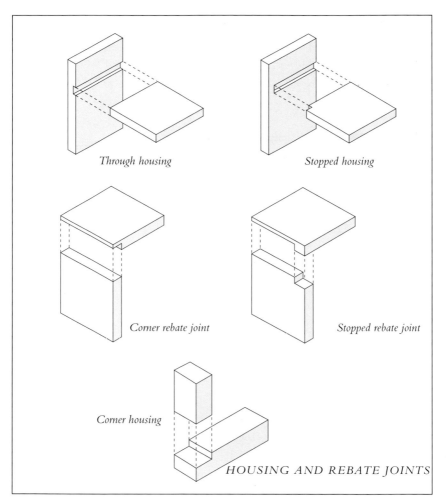

Through housing

Stopped housing

Corner rebate joint

Stopped rebate joint

Corner housing

HOUSING AND REBATE JOINTS

6 A housing joint may be secured by any one of the following methods, or by a combination of them:
• gluing and cramping until the adhesive is set
• screwing through the face of the outside piece
• dovetail nailing through the face of the outside piece
• skew nailing through in the corner

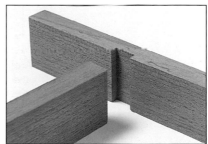

A housing joint is quite strong.

Barefaced tongue-and-groove joint

This is a combination of a housing joint and a rebate joint, the housing restricting the movement of the joint. It is used in furniture construction and window reveals.

CONSTRUCTION

1 Square the ends of both pieces of timber. Set out the shoulder line on the end of one piece (A), coming in from the end by the thickness of the other piece. Square across the face side and across both edges. This line is the barefaced side of the timber.

2 Square a second shoulder line back towards the end and across both edges. This should be spaced one-third the thickness of the timber.

3 Gauge the depth of the groove (one-third the thickness of the timber) on the edge between the two shoulder lines.

4 Cut the shoulders down to the gauge line with a tenon saw. Remove the waste with a narrow chisel and check for flatness.

5 With the gauge set as before, mark a line across the back face and across the edges of the other piece (B).

6 Gauge from the face side towards the end on each side and across the end. Saw down to both gauge lines with a tenon saw. Do not cut too deep, as this will weaken the joint.

7 Chisel in from the end to remove the waste. Check for fit and adjust the joint as necessary.

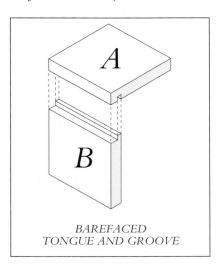

BAREFACED TONGUE AND GROOVE

HINTS
• Joints such as a barefaced tongue-and-groove joint can be easily constructed using a router and jig, either just for the groove or for both groove and rebate. See pages 30–1 for the correct techniques when using a router.
• If the fit of the tongue is a little tight, plane the face of the tongue to obtain a snug fit, or you can rub it with abrasive paper.

Halving joints

Halving or half-lap joints are framing joints used to join two pieces of timber (usually of equal thickness) on edge or on flat. The joint is constructed by removing equal amounts of timber from each piece so they finish flush on top and bottom.

TYPES OF HALVING JOINT

There are six main types: cross, tee, corner, mitre, dovetail and end. All are made in the same way: removing half the thickness from each piece.

• Cross halving joint. This is used to allow two pieces of timber to cross each other without having to cut one in half. The width is made to suit the width of the intersecting piece. Wood is removed from the top of one piece and the bottom of the other.

• Tee halving joint. This is made with laps that intersect at 90 degrees and can also be made as a stopped joint (not full width).

• Corner halving joint. Similar to a tee halving, but both parts can be cut with a tenon saw.

• Mitre halving joint. This can be used when the top face of the timber has a moulding on it. By mitring the top of the halving, the mould returns around the corner.

• Dovetail halving joint. This tee halving joint has a wedge (dovetail) cut on the lap, either both sides or on one side. The joint will only come apart if the top piece is lifted out of the socket. The pitch for the dovetail is usually 1:6.

• End halving joint (scarf halving). This joint is used to join timber end to end by overlapping the two pieces. The length of the overlap is equal to the width of the timber. The joint requires some support for it to have any strength.

CONSTRUCTING A CORNER HALVING JOINT

1 Square the ends of both pieces of timber. Square a line across the top face of one piece, coming in the width of the other. Repeat on the underside of the other piece. Square the lines down the edges of both pieces of timber.

2 Set a marking gauge to half the thickness of the timber and mark a line around the ends and both edges of both pieces. Mark the waste, on the top of one piece and the bottom of the other.

3 Hold the timber on end in a vice at 45 degrees. Saw down the waste side of the centre line until the cut reaches the diagonal point. Turn the timber around and continue cutting while gradually lifting the handle of

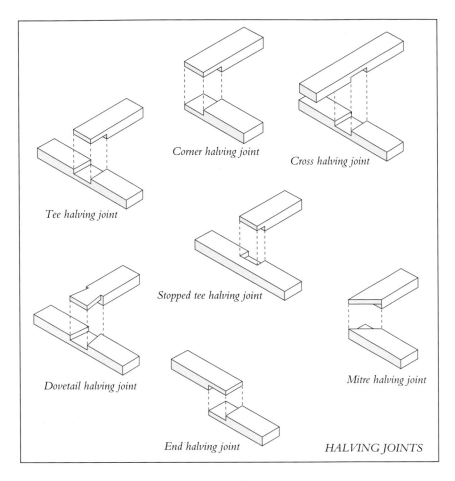

Corner halving joint

Cross halving joint

Tee halving joint

Stopped tee halving joint

Dovetail halving joint

Mitre halving joint

End halving joint

HALVING JOINTS

the saw until the cut reaches the shoulder line on both edges.

4 Remove the timber from the vice and lay flat. Hold it firmly against a bench hook or cramp it down.

5 Cut the shoulder to the first saw cut and remove the waste. Any unevenness in the lap should be cleaned out with a paring chisel or shoulder plane. Check for flatness.

6 Repeat the cutting on the other piece of timber.

7 Check the two pieces fit together and adjust as necessary with a paring chisel. The joint should be square, flush, and have no gaps.

8 The joint must be glued and may be strengthened with screws or nails. Alternatively, glue two dowels through the joint and pare off.

Mitre joints

A mitre joint is used at corners to hide the end grain and so that a moulded shape can continue around a corner.

TYPES OF MITRE JOINT

To create a mitre, the angle at which two surfaces meet is bisected. In a true mitre, this is 90 degrees and so each surface is cut to 45 degrees, but the angle may be obtuse or acute. Mitre joints are commonly used for picture frames, for joining architrave, skirtings, coving, dado and picture rails and for fitting beading into glazed doors.

CONSTRUCTING A TRUE MITRE

1 Set out the length of the material, keeping in mind that if the mitre is inside a corner, the length is measured on the long face of the mitre. If the mitre is on the outside of a corner, the length is measured on the short face but allow for the thickness of the material.

2 Once the length has been determined, mark a 45 degree line on the edge or face where the angle is to be cut.

3 Using a combination or try square, square a line across each side of the timber.

4 To cut the timber by hand, use a mitre box with a fine-toothed saw such as a tenon saw. Hold the work firmly against the back of the mitre box when cutting: if it slips, it will result in an uneven cut and a poorly-fitting joint. You will need packing under the workpiece as mitre box slots do not go all the way to the bottom. If cutting freehand, take care to follow the set-out lines on all sides of the work. The best results will be obtained with a metal mitre saw; most have cramps to hold the workpiece.

5 Place the two pieces together and check the fit. You may be able to adjust it by planing the surface of the mitre. Hold the work firmly and use a fine-set, sharp block plane.

6 If the joint is to be nailed, start the nails in both pieces by laying them flat and nailing through the external face until the point just comes through the mitred face.

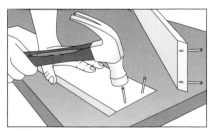

6 Start the nails in both pieces, nailing until the point just comes through the mitred face.

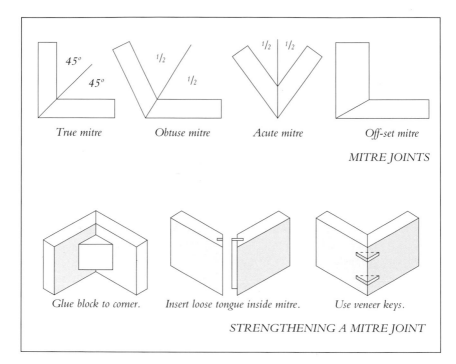

True mitre   *Obtuse mitre*   *Acute mitre*   *Off-set mitre*

MITRE JOINTS

Glue block to corner.   *Insert loose tongue inside mitre.*   *Use veneer keys.*

STRENGTHENING A MITRE JOINT

7 Apply adhesive and hold the joint firmly, with one side slightly overlapping the other. Drive the nails in the overlapping side first. As the nails are driven in, the weight of the hammer will cause the joint to slip. When the nails are driven home, the surfaces should line up. Nail the other side and punch the nails home.

8 If you have a small gap because your mitre does not quite line up, rub over the open corner of the joint from both sides with the round shaft of a screwdriver. This will push the fibres over on the outside and perhaps hide the gap. If the gap is too wide, however, you may have to make it good with a filler.

9 To add strength to a mitre joint, you may glue a block on the inside as long as it is not seen. If appearance is important, a loose tongue placed inside the joint or veneer keys, applied from the outside, for example when constructing a box, across the joint will give extra strength.

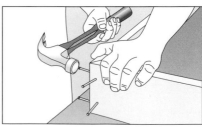

7 Drive the nails in the overlapping side first as the weight of the hammer will cause the joint to pull up.

Scarf and scribe joints

A scarf joint joins timber end to end, whilst a scribe joint is used where one piece of moulded timber is butted against another.

SCARF JOINTS

A true scarf joint joins timber end to end with bevels cut on the end of each piece of timber so that uniform thickness is maintained. This joint is mainly used for joining frames longer than the available timber length.

SCRIBE JOINTS

A scribe joint is used where one piece of timber with a moulded or irregular shape, such as an ogee skirting or cove moulding, is butted against another in a corner. The timber can be moved back while it is being fixed and any gap that may appear is less noticeable than with a mitre joint.

1 Fix the first moulding in place. Butt the end of the other piece against the fixed moulding, keeping it in alignment.

2 Slide a small block of timber and sharp pencil together over the surface of the fixed moulding. The pencil will mark (scribe) a line on the face of the moulding to be fitted.

3 Cut along the scribed line. Check the fit and adjust as necessary.

DETAILED MOULDINGS

Put the first piece in place and use a mitre box or mitre saw to cut a mitre on the end of the other piece. The line formed by the moulded face and mitre will show the shape needed. Cut along this line with a fret saw.

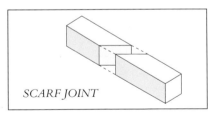

SCARF JOINT

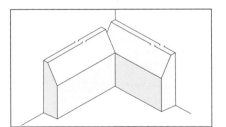

1 Fix the first moulding in place and butt the other piece against it, keeping it in alignment.

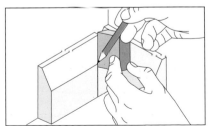

2 Slide a block of timber and a pencil together over the surface of the fixed moulding, marking the second piece.

Mortise-and-tenon joints

The mortise-and-tenon joint is used in framing where two pieces of timber meet at a corner or intersection. It is probably the strongest of all the framing joints used in woodworking and is used to construct doors, windows and furniture.

TYPES OF JOINT

The two main types are the common mortise-and-tenon joint, and the haunched mortise-and-tenon joint.

The haunched mortise-and-tenon joint is used at corners. The mortise-and-tenon are reduced to about two-thirds of the width of the material. A haunch (shoulder) is left next to the tenon and fits into a small recess near the mortise. The haunch helps prevent the rail twisting.

COMMON MORTISE-AND-TENON JOINT

1 Locate the position for the joint on both pieces of timber and square these marks around the timber. The marks represent the width of each intersecting piece. The tenon will be on the end of the rail and the mortise will be through the stile. A little waste should be left on the end of the tenon for cleaning up the joint.

2 Select a chisel that is as close as possible to one-third the thickness of the material. Set a mortise gauge to the same width as the chisel and gauge the mortise in the middle of the stile between the set out lines. Work from the face side. If you prefer, use a marking gauge set to one-third of the thickness of the stile and work from both faces.

3 In the same way, gauge the tenon at the end and down both sides to the shoulder lines on the rail.

4 Start by drilling out the mortise, using a drill bit slightly smaller than the width of the mortise—and, preferably, using a vertical drill stand to keep the drill on line. Since what you are doing is basically removing material, you can drill from both sides.

5 Place a support piece of timber in the vice, high enough to cramp the stile on edge. Cramp the stile to the support piece close to the set out on the mortise.

6 Chisel the mortise, starting about 3 mm from each end, being sure not to damage the end of the mortise when levering out the waste. Be sure to chisel straight by keeping the blade parallel to the face of the stile. Lever out the waste. Continue down about half way through. Turn the timber over and come in from the other side in the same manner.

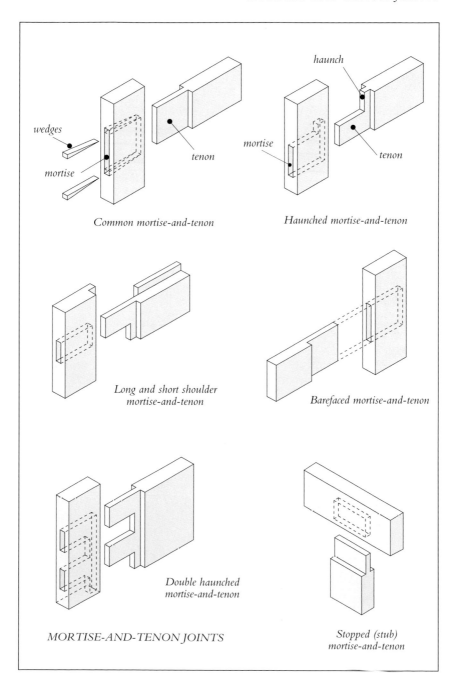

Common mortise-and-tenon

Haunched mortise-and-tenon

Long and short shoulder
mortise-and-tenon

Barefaced mortise-and-tenon

Double haunched
mortise-and-tenon

Stopped (stub)
mortise-and-tenon

MORTISE-AND-TENON JOINTS

7 Once the bulk of the waste has been removed, clean the mortise and cut back to the set out lines by paring straight in from each side.

8 Cut the tenon, cutting on the waste side of the line and cut the shoulders with a tenon saw.

9 Test for fit and adjust as required. The shoulders of the tenon should fit neatly against the stile and finish square and free of twist.

10 To lock the joint, wedges may be placed on both sides of the tenon. The clearance for these is made in the mortise: from the outside of the stile, chisel the ends of the mortise about two-thirds of the way through at a slope of 1:8. The wedges are cut at the same slope. Alternatively, saw cuts can be made in the tenon and wedges driven into them.

11 Glue the joint and cramp it up tight. Check for square. Apply adhesive to the wedges and drive in firmly. Saw off the excess wedge, plane off any exposed tenon and clean up the adhesive when set.

OTHER MORTISE-AND-TENON JOINTS
Mortise-and-tenon joints for sash and door construction differ slightly from the haunched mortise-and-tenon, although the technique for constructing them is the same. A rebate and/or a moulding is run on the inside to take the glass or panel.

When making a mortise-and-tenon joint in timber that has a rebate on it, keep the face of the tenon in line with the edge of the rebate. One shoulder on the rail is left longer (by the depth of the rebate) and the other short to fit against the top of the rebate—hence the name long and short shoulder mortise-and-tenon joint.

Mortise-and-tenon joints for timber with mouldings have a scribed shoulder to match the moulding. Alternatively, you can remove the moulding from the edge of the mortise and mitre or scribe it to match the corresponding piece.

Other types of mortise-and-tenon joints are:
• barefaced—for timbers of different thicknesses
• double haunched—for wider sections of timber such as door bottom rails

All these joints may be stopped, (stub), so that no end grain is seen on the outside of the stile, or they can be wedged and pinned.

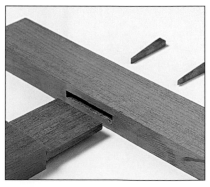

Wedges can be used for a neat fit.

Bridle joints

A bridle joint is used where two pieces of timber meet on edge, either at a corner or an intersection (for example, the corner of a window or where a table leg meets a rail).

TYPES OF BRIDLE JOINT

A bridle joint is very similar to a mortise-and-tenon joint. The most common types are the corner bridle and the tee bridle. This type of joint relies mainly on adhesive for strength but it may have timber dowels inserted through the joint to give it added strength.

BRIDLE JOINT

1 Set out as for a mortise-and-tenon joint (see steps 1–4 on page 64), anddivide the thickness of the material by three to find one-third. Mark the waste on both pieces. On one piece, the centre will need to be removed. On the other, each outside piece will need to be removed.

2 Cut all the pieces to the shoulder line on the waste side. On the rail, cut the shoulders with a tenon saw to reveal the pin.

3 Working from both sides, remove the waste from the stile socket with a mortise chisel or coping saw.

4 Check for fit; adjust as necessary with a chisel. Apply adhesive to the surface of the joint. Check for square. Use a G-cramp to hold the joint while the adhesive sets.

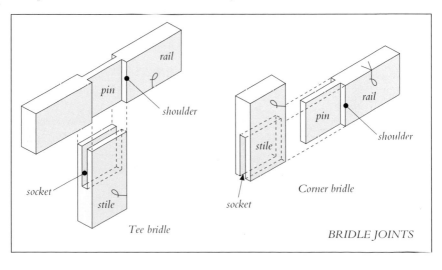

rail

pin

shoulder

socket

stile

Tee bridle

rail

pin

shoulder

stile

socket

Corner bridle

BRIDLE JOINTS

Widening joints

Wide, good-quality timber is becoming harder to obtain and is very expensive. These wide boards are also prone to excessive movement, making them difficult to work. Widening joints are used to join narrower boards together on edge to create a wide panel for table or bench tops and panelling in doors.

PREPARATION

Before you begin to construct a widening joint you need to follow certain procedures:

• Select quarter sawn timber where possible. It is less prone to movement across the face than plain sawn timber. If plain sawn boards are used, place them with the heart sides on alternate surfaces. Any movement will be minimised as the boards will support each other.

• Avoid putting quarter and plain sawn boards together in the same panel as they will have different amounts of movement.

• Never mix different species of timber if they aren't seasoned (dried) properly. They will move at different rates and this will split either the joint or the timber.

• If possible, arrange all the pieces so the grain lies in one direction. This will be a help when planing.

• Always bring the timber to its correct size before jointing.

• Always use a good quality adhesive (see page 70).

• Match any grain or colour in the timber if the work is to be polished.

WIDENING BUTT JOINT

1 Lay all the pieces out with the face up. To help match the pieces up later, mark the edges to be joined with a continuous pencil line across the joints at an angle. Alternatively, you can number each one.

2 Plane the edges true and test for fit against the corresponding pieces. Line the ends or the pencil lines up each time.

3 Check that there is no gap and the surface is flat. If you try to close gaps with a clamp or by filling them, the joint will split later.

4 If planing short lengths, place both pieces in the vice face to face and plane both edges together. The edges do not have to be square as the angles will complement each other.

5 Prepare the joint as for a butt joint (see page 52) and apply adhesive. For smaller sections, a rubbed adhesive joint using polyvinyl acetate (PVA) may be satisfactory. Other adhesives will need to be clamped. Rub the

two surfaces together with a downward pressure, forcing out the excess adhesive and creating a suction between the surfaces.

OTHER WIDENING JOINTS

Other widening joints reinforced for extra strength and alignment are prepared the same way. They include:

- dowelled edge joint
- tongue–and–groove joints
- rebate joint

A loose tongue–and–groove joint.

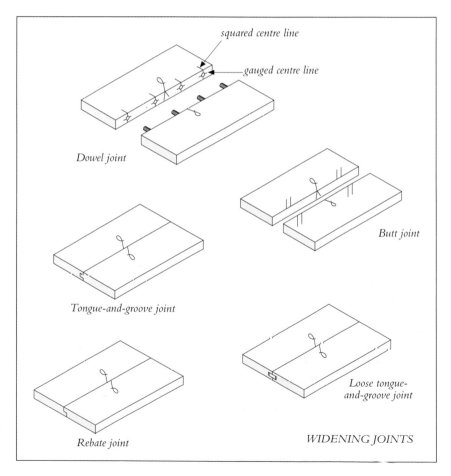

squared centre line

gauged centre line

Dowel joint

Butt joint

Tongue-and-groove joint

Loose tongue-and-groove joint

Rebate joint

WIDENING JOINTS

Gluing and cramping

Gluing and cramping are an important part of the woodworker's work, without which many items would lack strength.

ADHESIVES

Adhesive adds strength to the job by holding the work fast so that it cannot be pulled apart easily. Always wear protective gloves when working with adhesives and follow instructions on the package for safe use. Clean excess adhesive off the job before it sets as it can blunt plane blades and clog up sanding paper.

PVA (POLYVINYL ACETATE)

PVA is a common general-purpose woodworking adhesive. While still wet, it can be wiped off with a damp cloth. It has excellent gap-filling properties and needs cramping for a short time only. It sets in about an hour. PVA is quite strong and will adhere to almost any porous surface. It bonds permanently but is not heat or water resistant. Apply it to joints with a brush, but for larger flat surfaces dilute it with water and apply with a roller. Being water-based, PVA will shrink while it is setting.

CONTACT ADHESIVE

Contact adhesive bonds on contact. Apply it to both surfaces and when it is touch dry place them together. It is used to bond plastic laminate or veneer to chipboard. No cramping is required. It cleans off with thinners.

Contact adhesive is flammable. Use it in a well-ventilated area to reduce the effects of the fumes. It is not recommended for outside use as it is not waterproof or heatproof.

EPOXY ADHESIVE

Epoxy adhesive is the strongest woodworking adhesive and the most expensive. A two-part resin adhesive, it does not shrink as it sets and will not soften with heat or creep under load. It is waterproof and bonds most materials, porous or not, except thermoplastic (PVC or perspex). It is suitable for outside use. It will clean up with thinners when wet.

HOT-MELT ADHESIVE

Hot melt adhesive bonds almost anything, including many plastics. It generally comes as a stick that is inserted into an electric glue gun. Apply it, press the work together and hold for 30 seconds. No cramping is needed. It cleans up with thinners.

CRAMPS

Cramps come in a wide range of styles and sizes, but the most useful are the adjustable quick-action cramp, similar trigger cramp, G-cramp, pipe cramp and sash cramp used for large boards or frames.

Always place a small scrap of timber between the jaws and the work to prevent bruising the timber when pressure is applied.

GLUING AND CRAMPING TECHNIQUES

Before gluing any project make a trial assembly without adhesive. Cramp it if necessary to check the joints and the overall size.

If all is correct, pull the project apart, keeping the pieces in order. Set up the gluing area with cramps already set out to the correct width.

ASSEMBLING A FRAME

Using a brush for even cover, spread adhesive on both sides of the joint and assemble the work quickly. Wipe off excess adhesive and place the job in the cramps. Apply an even pressure to close the joints. The cramps should be square and parallel to the work.

Keep the cramps as close as possible to the joint. Check the rails are parallel and adjust as necessary. Measure the diagonals: if they are the same, the job is square. If not, a sharp tap on the end of the stile may move it. If necessary adjust the cramps.

If the work is not flat across the surface, tap any parts that are kicked up with a mallet and block of timber. If this fails, you may need to ease off the cramps or to cramp a block of timber across the job.

ASSEMBLING A PANEL

Using a brush, apply an even coat of adhesive on both edges. Position a cramp at each end of the job and no more than 300 mm apart. Check the ends are flush and pencil marks align. Apply light pressure with the cramps. A cramp over the top will even up pressure and help prevent cupping.

Tighten the cramps evenly. Remove excess adhesive and allow the job to dry. Ensure the surface is flat, flush and free of twist.

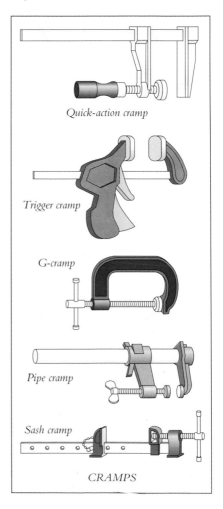

Quick-action cramp

Trigger cramp

G-cramp

Pipe cramp

Sash cramp

CRAMPS

Index